WYANF   828

JC¹

THE MIDLIFE
MANUAL

THE MIDLIFE
MANUAL

JOHN O'CONNELL & JESSICA CARGILL THOMPSON

CB

First published in 2010 by
Short Books
3A Exmouth House
Pine Street
EC1R 0JH

10 9 8 7 6 5 4 3 2 1

A CIP catalogue record for this book is
available from the British Library.

ISBN 978-1-907595-05-9

Printed in Great Britain by Clays, Suffolk

Design: Georgia Vaux

Twitter: @welcomemidlife

FIRST, A QUESTIONNAIRE. ARE YOU:

a) Aged between 40 and 55?

b) Acutely conscious that life hasn't panned out for you quite the way you thought it would when you were 18?

c) Obsessed by your childhood, especially your inability to remember it?

d) Alienated by technology?

e) Scared of cancer?

f) Even more scared of death?

g) Planning your retirement, even though you know it's going to be a wasteland of impoverished misery?

h) Nervous of all the young people in your office?

i) A lot happier when you've had a couple of glasses of wine?

j) Okay, half a bottle?

k) Getting divorced?

l) Consoling friends who are getting divorced?

m) Having, or considering having, an affair?

n) Having, or considering having, an affair with friends who are getting divorced?

o) Aware that The Beatles were only in their late twenties when they split up? They'd made all those records, records that changed the world. And what have you achieved? *What?*

p) Worrying about what all those drugs you took when you were younger are going to do to you?

q) Stuck with a tattoo you hate?

r) Tired. Just really, really tired?

s) And depressed?

t) And angry. Christ, where does that anger come from? Why did no one prepare you for it?

u) 'Growing out' of all your clothes?

v) Thinking about moving to the country?

w) Turning into your parents?

x) Puzzled because you seem, somewhere along the line, to have lost all the friends you actually liked and acquired a load of new ones you barely know?

y) Constantly obsessing about accessorising your home?

z) Aware that noticing, and moreover having opinions about, 'stuff in the papers' marks you out as practically dead?

If you've answered 'yes' to more than half of these questions, then congratulations, you are officially experiencing 'midlife'. Middle age. The *beginning of the end*. Do not worry. Help is at hand...

CONTENTS

1.
PERSONAL DEVELOPMENT

The older we get, the more enthusiastically we embrace change. But this change is a double-edged thing. We acquire wisdom, but also the temper of Zeus. We learn how to make the world's tastiest Christmas cake, but forget our friends' names unless they're written down.

RADICAL CHEEK

When you were younger you were so damn radical you refused to eat South African apples; you had a day out in London c/o your student union to march against student loans; you refused to pay the poll tax; handcuffed yourself to pop stars to protest against Section 28; you camped at Greenham and once even threw a sickie so you could take part in an anti-capitalist march, though only because a really cute girl you met in a bar said she was going too.

While no one can accuse you of lacking fighting spirit, it is nevertheless the case that, nowadays, this has been redirected into causes such as: arguing with your line manager; arguing with your parents; arguing with the call-centre drone dealing with your broadband; arguing with the traffic warden who has just given you a ticket for parking your people mover on the zigzags outside school when you were only dropping your kids off *for fuck's sake* and you had to be quick because you had a hair appointment.

But at least you buy Fair Trade bananas, and you signed the online petition about the planned bypass *and* you really do feel quite bad about buying cheap clothes you know have been stitched by tiny hands. And only last week you nearly didn't buy cod because you saw a documentary about over-fishing...

See? Still an activist at heart.

ANGER MANAGEMENT

Getting older is a licence to be angry. About anything – the more trivial the better. And once we start, we can't stop.

One minute we are carefree 20-year-olds, oblivious to the minor worries of the world around us; the next we are posting strongly worded threats on internet discussion forums about our neighbours' wheelie bins. But doesn't it feel good? The rising pulse, the adrenalin rush, the dilated pupils... It's a bit like the last time you took E.

Untrustworthy, anecdotal evidence gathered from the discussion forum thread postings of our fellow south London residents suggests the topics most likely to raise the average midlifer's blood pressure are:

- speed bumps
- antisocial people having house parties
- the unsightliness of decaying road
accident flowers
- schools being closed for elections/
snow/gas leaks
- toddlers weeing in the street
- aeroplane noise
- foxes chewing through the pipes of
garden watering systems, then pooing on
your doorstep
- an unidentified loud humming noise
- the price of petrol
- other people's security lights

Why is it bad to get angry in midlife?
- It increases your risk of having a heart attack. Researchers at Johns Hopkins School of Medicine tracked 1,055 medical students for 36 years. They found that the angry ones were six times more likely to suffer a heart attack by the age of 55 and three times more likely to develop heart or blood vessel disease. (No, we don't know how the researchers measured their subjects' anger. Number of plates thrown per month?)

• Anger reduces your attention span. When you're angry, a surge in brain chemicals like norepinephrine and cortisol makes you 'hyperfocus', as if you were stalking a deer through a forest. Which you wouldn't be, ever, obviously. But you know, it's an attractive image.

• It will come to define you, and not in a sexy way like 'angry young man'. 'Angry old man' merely evokes the smell of dandruff and old slippers.

WHEN CHEESE IS MORE THAN JUST CHEESE...

It isn't just wine that inspires nerdish levels of food snobbery. Seemingly proletarian commodities are also open to exploitation by the midlifer intent on a bit of gastronomic one-upmanship. The joy, of course, is to revel in the endless variety available within an innocuous category of foodstuff like 'tea' or 'cheese'; the challenge is to find the most obscure and hard-to-source example, even if it tastes like old socks.

Cheese

With more than 700 varieties of cheese produced in the UK alone and nearly 400 in France, there is scope for indulgence of trainspotterish proportions as you work your way along the cheese counter. Try to restrain yourself from 'theming' your cheese board, however, eg only cheeses from Wales (Caerphilly, Snowdonia, Y-Fenni) or beginning with the letter V (Vacherin, Blue Vinney, Vignotte). This will make you look like you have too much time on your hands.

Whether you actually serve your cheese course before or after what you used to call pudding but now call dessert isn't in itself important; merely to know that conflicting schools of thought exist is enough.

Feel free to make a fuss in any restaurant that neglects to give your cheeseboard time to reach room temperature or provide a different knife for each cheese to avoid contamination of flavours. Cross off your Christmas card list any guest uncouth enough to cut the point (or 'nose') off the Brie.

Chocolate

Annoy any obsessive dieters by going on about how chocolate is actually really good for you and not at all fattening if you go for the good stuff with more than 70% cocoa (ie less than 30% fat). Stress that, by raising levels of serotonin (responsible for happy feelings) in the brain, it can lower blood pressure and has even been shown – 'by scientists' – to ward off cancer.

Insist on tasting all chocolate by snapping it ostentatiously (a good 'snap' signifies quality product), then placing it towards the back of your tongue to melt. Mutter stuff about being able to detect berries, smoky notes and a long finish. In fact, employ any wine vocab you might have picked up – it's all valid.

Meanwhile, make sure you haven't left any Wispa wrappers visible in the bin.

Honey

With honey, it's important to bang on self-righteously about antioxidants and amino acids. Roll out with conviction old wives' tales about local honey being a natural defence against hay fever as you are building up resistance to the pollen by ingesting it. Remember to mention the plight of the bee vis-à-vis potential ecological catastrophe.

Insist on keeping at least three types of honey on the go at any one time, explaining to guests how 'the lavender honey tastes so very different from the heather honey, it's practically a different foodstuff!'

Tea

Why offer guests a mere 'cup of tea' when names such as Orange Pekoe, Imperial Oolong, Darjeeling, Lapsang Souchong and Silver Needle trip so silkily off the tongue? The leaves and buds of the *Camellia sinensis*, handpicked, can be categorised as: green tea (the earliest form of tea, unoxidised); blue tea (semi-oxidised); black tea (the strongest and most familiar to Western palates); white teas (the rarest and most delicate).

Of course, it's not just about knowing what to drink but how to drink it. George Orwell once wrote an entire essay on the subject for the *Evening Standard*. Favouring strong Indian teas over Chinese, his eleven golden rules, since you ask, included using loose tea, a teapot, skimmed milk, and no sugar. As for the controversial matter of whether to put the milk in first...

Q. A funny thing keeps happening to me. I'll hear a pop song from my childhood that I wasn't aware I liked or even knew very well and suddenly I'll be a blubbing wreck. If I'm in a café or shop I'll have to go and hide in the toilet until the moment has passed. But it's no good because this emotional memory (if that's the phrase) will have triggered a torrent of other associations – the taste of a block of vanilla ice cream wedged between two salty wafers; the 'M' in the centre of the steering wheel of the Morris Minor my mum used to drive... What's going on?

A. Ah, yes. This is nostalgia – an emotion scientists believe is unique to humans. The word derives from the Greek 'nostos' (returning home) and 'algos' (pain or ache). The Victorians linked it to melancholia and suicide. We use it to denote a naïve idealisation of the past. But really it's more than that: a yearning to return to the world of your youth. Some psychologists think nostalgia is a clever attempt by our brains to protect us from the loneliness and isolation that comes with ageing. But we don't know any psychologists personally, so we can't verify that. It sounds plausible though, doesn't it?

AVERSION THERAPY: MAKE NOSTALGIA A THING OF THE PAST!

Nostalgia for your childhood

Sit down with some meat paste sandwiches and a bottle of Vimto and spend the day watching reruns of **Bread** on Dave, and leafing through a broadsheet newspaper with tiny type and no pictures of celebrities. Ask a friend to chain smoke next to you as you do this. Children of the 1970s should flick the mains switch off for about an hour just when you'd normally be cooking supper or watching TV. If you go out for a drink in the evening, be sure to leave the pub by 10.30pm. On no account turn your computer on.

Nostalgia for student days

Take £20 out of the cashpoint to live on for the week. Dig out your copy of *Brain Salad Surgery* by Emerson Lake & Palmer. Try to read the whole of *Paradise Lost* in one day. Pour beer over your carpet and leave to dry. Food: accessorise pasta with supermarket own-brand jar of pasta sauce that tastes like bile mixed with red custard. Otherwise just eat toast. On no account eat a vegetable.

Costume-drama-induced nostalgia

Costume dramas and country-house novels have become bywords for cosy cultural consumption, harking back to simple times when life seemed so much more straightforward. But as you wallow in your romanticising of *Lark Rise to Candleford*, Jane Austen, PG Wodehouse, *Foyle's War* or Agatha Christie, remember that as well as featuring pretty hamlets and unspoilt countryside, balls in Bath, hilarious public-school japes in country houses, the wearing of hats and dressing for pre-dinner cocktails, they were also times of poverty, disease and hard manual labour, extreme sexual inequality, extreme social inequality, war and murder (the latter usually in country houses at cocktail hour by over-privileged people in hats).

Nostalgia for lost loves

Google them or look them up on Facebook. See how saggy/paunchy/ mumsy/bald they've become. Believe it or not, the brooding youth or foxy JCR social sec whose soft-focus image you've carried in your head all these years is now as creased and careworn as you are. (NB Any old flames who appear to have become successful lawyers, celebrated novelists, fighter pilots or supermodels must obviously be completely different people who just coincidentally share the same name. And background. And look a bit similar.)

FOOD YOU REALLY SHOULD HAVE GROWN OUT OF BY NOW

pickled onion Monster Munch
instant noodles
ketchup with everything
yoghurt you suck out of tubes
sugar-coated cereals
blue drinks
Slush Puppies
processed-potato smiley faces
99 Flakes
alcopops
fizzy cola bottles and exploding sherbert
tinned spaghetti (especially if in amusing shapes or containing mini sausages)

FOOD YOU REALLY SHOULD HAVE LEARNT TO LIKE BY NOW

olives
oysters
sushi
haggis
herbal tea
salty liquorice
neat spirits
real ale
rare steak
kale
sweetbreads
anchovies
eels
celery
mushrooms
seemingly weird combinations like strawberries + basil, or pepper chocolate
sweet things in savoury dishes
flowers in salads
beetroot
really smelly cheese
walnuts
Guinness
Christmas pudding

'WE MUST MEET UP FOR A DRINK!'

Just to be clear – a six-monthly text or email exchange in which you say 'we must meet up for a drink' is not the same as *actually* meeting up for a drink.

ISN'T IT IRONIC...

In your teens and twenties, it seemed impossibly funny to say the opposite of what you meant or knew to be true. It fitted nicely with the posture of cynical, dissenting sophistication you felt obliged to adopt and made you look... clever? Was that what it was? (That, by the way, is the title of a song by the ironic Pet Shop Boys, a band you liked a lot at the time for their posture of cynical, dissenting sophistication.)

The problem with irony is all the things it doesn't allow you to do – to be sincere, for example, or to emote in any way, emotion being so easily confused with sentimentality. And this just isn't sustainable into your thirties and forties when, whether you like it or not, stuff will erupt into your life which only a psychopath would attempt to tackle in a spirit of lofty detachment.

Also, you no longer have time to waste watching crap like *Big Brother*, which you used to say you were watching ironically when, ironically, you weren't. If you really *were* to start watching it ironically then that would be doubly wasteful of the time you no longer have – if you see what we mean.

DEAR GOD...

You've always called yourself an atheist. You bought that Richard Dawkins book and loved the sound of little faith-grapes being splattered by the mallet of scientific fundamentalism. But then, shortly after your 48th birthday, something weird happened. You started to worry. About what would happen if, you know, there *was actually a God*.

What if you were waiting in line to go through the turnstile into heaven when suddenly you felt St Peter's bony fingers on your arm – 'Come on, lad. What's through there isn't for you.'

'But it must be! I can see my parents! They're smiling and beckoning!'

'I'm sure they are, son.'

'I must go to them.'

'There's no "must" about it.'

'What do you mean?'

'It's the Dawkins Room for you. You might want to take off that cardigan...'

One night, in the sweaty course of which you dreamed a dream very much along these lines, you resolved to start going to church. Not all the time. Just... occasionally. And in secret. Because your children – the children you taught from an early age that only stupid people believed in God – would campaign for the stocks to be brought back just so they *could put you in them and throw rotten fruit at you* if they got the merest inkling.

The problem with the whole religion-as-insurance-policy approach is that God is omniscient: He knows what you're up to and you're still going to fry.

FRIENDS REUNITED

The curse of Facebook means it's easier than ever to organise reunions. If you're on it – and you shouldn't be, because it's for children – you're contactable, and if you're not, well, there's always some Judas who knows where you live and is willing to pass on the information. Subtly different are the formal reunions masterminded by your old school or university. With their gilt-edged invitations promising marquees and sun-dappled lawns, they're slightly more tempting and you may feel yourself wavering. *Maybe it would be fun? I could stay in my old room!*

Now, this is a ridiculous notion. One: your 'old room' was a hole, which seemed okay at the time only because it was bigger than the box room at home and had a fire and a toaster. Two: if you felt any kind of warmth towards your alma mater, you'd have visited it before now and wouldn't keep binning all those letters begging for donations.

So the only incentive for attendance is a desperate, ghoulish hope that the lives of the people who made you miserable will have spiralled out of control, and that everyone looks older, fatter and more tired than you. This isn't a bad incentive, as incentives go. However:

- Don't assume that people who were failures at school are failures as middle-aged adults. This is not how the world works.
- Wait a decent amount of time – 20 minutes at least – before breaking away from your partner to go in search of an old boyfriend or girlfriend.
- Don't keep saying, 'It's been so long, I can't think why we haven't been in touch…' when you know perfectly well.
- Don't begin conversations by asking, 'So what do you do now?' You'll still be there half an hour later. Try a more lateral approach, for example: 'How many funerals have you been to in the past year?'
- Allow your eyes a maximum of two seconds' 'resting time' on any part of a

person's anatomy. This is just long enough to allow you to take in baldness and fatness and assess the amount of work someone has had done without it being too obvious.

- Don't ask about children. Just don't.
- When the guy who was a failure at school but is now a Drama Producer for Radio 4 reveals this fact to you, don't say, 'That's an amazing coincidence because do you know I've just written a play for radio! It's called "What's Good for the Goose" and it's set on a farm in Cumbria in the run-up to Christmas. I've got it here actually, on a little flash drive...'

MIDLIFE MISCONCEPTION:
THAT THE INDULGENCE OF ECCENTRICITIES IS ACCEPTABLE

So you want to walk around the house with no clothes on? What of it? You're 47; it's your house. If someone knocks at the door and you answer it and they're shocked, well – tough. Being naked in your own home isn't public nudity. It isn't indecent. You've looked into this and the legal definition of indecency is 'conduct that the average man would find shocking and revolting'.

The average man (maybe even woman – you haven't told your wife or daughters about it) has much more important things to worry about. And while your body isn't what it used to be, seeing it unclad isn't going to make anyone spontaneously vomit.

So – let's have no more of this nonsense.

Of course, there were always going to be remarks made about your hair. And you admit it's an unusual style – shoulder-length; dyed black; a line shaved through the centre parting. You've tried explaining its, er, genesis (it was a look sported by Peter Gabriel in the early 1970s), but even among fans of melodic but intense art-rock made by Old Carthusians the response has been lukewarm. Someone said it looked 'satanic'. But that's just stupid, isn't it? Satan doesn't have hair.

- -

THINGS THAT PASS FOR EXCITEMENT THESE DAYS

A double espresso

A new organic café opening on your high street

The arrival of the new Boden catalogue

Finishing *Wolf Hall*

General elections

A bountiful tomato harvest from your growbag

Successful erection of flat-pack furniture

Being out in town after 11.30pm

Finding out someone famous has moved in across the street from you

Cupcakes

The fact that there's an Argos iPhone app

The idea that there might possibly be new albums at some point from Kate Bush or David Bowie or the remaining members of Pink Floyd

Losing 2lb

Beating a younger colleague at squash

A racy storyline in *The Archers*

The first of the season's asparagus in your veg box

Ordering dessert

FRIENDSHIP: MALE

Men are rubbish at making and keeping friends because they don't work hard enough at it. As a result, by the time you get to midlife your social circle consists of:

1 your partner's friends, assuming you have a partner and that this partner is female

2 the ghosts of people you used to be friends with when you worked with them and to whom you still refer as 'friends' even though you haven't seen them in eight years. To be honest, you wouldn't know how to get in touch with them if you wanted to. Except through Facebook. And you're not doing *that*. What are you, desperate?

3 a couple of old friends from school who you see once or twice a year and have nothing in common with beyond the fact of your shared past and, possibly, an ability to reproduce.

4 a couple of old friends from university – people you saw a lot of just after you'd graduated but drifted more or less completely out of touch with because:

a) you disliked their partners
b) you were jealous of their jobs
c) you secretly fancied them and it all got a bit intense
d) you realised they were stealing from you to fund an out-of-control coke habit
e) you realised their manic 'high-spiritedness' (their phrase) was a symptom of bipolarity and decided to withdraw quietly because clinically depressed friends are exhausting – you already had three of them when two is the most anyone can cope with
f) they were once present when you were so drunk that you wet yourself
g) they admitted they had always voted Tory, way before voting Tory was something people did simply because there wasn't a plausible alternative

h) they droned on and on about their role in the Britpop War of 1995–96 (junior press officer for a tiny Camden-based indie label) as if it was actually a proper war that they and their muppety, drugged-up colleagues were trying to win

i) they kept telling you, when you did meet, that The Office wasn't funny, couldn't possibly be funny, because situation comedy reached an unsurpassable high with Blackadder II in 1985

5 the random collection of actors, photographers, builders and antiques dealers you spend every weekend with travelling to provincial towns to watch your team being subjected to another humiliating defeat. You think of these people as your 'family', partly because of the intense emotional experiences you share, but mainly because you see far more of them than you do your actual family.

6 'Dave Shuffle', 'One Eyed Jack', 'The Bluffer' and 'Chelmsford John' from the online poker forum.

7 The dog.

- -

FRIENDSHIP: FEMALE

As you think nothing of striking up a conversation with the person next to you in a queue, overcompensate for feeling isolated and/or having a boring job by joining local committees and book groups, and always make time to send Christmas cards and update your blog with your child's every acheievement or your latest emotional hiccup, by now you have a HUGE circle of friends. The fact that you haven't actually seen many of these people face to face for several years or had a conversation of longer than five minutes (not including talking about your work/their children/schools) is immaterial.

Your extensive social circle consists of:

1 all the brilliant, supportive women you've met on the internet

2 the summer fair committee

3 the parents of the children at school you want your own children to be friends with, which is why you are always inviting these children over for playdates

4 the parents of the children at school that your children are actually friends with, largely because they have bigger gardens, more video games, and parents who feed them reconstituted potato shapes for tea

5 work colleagues. And ex-work colleagues. And partners of work colleagues, particularly your line manager because if you're nice to her perhaps she'll let you take the afternoon off for sport's day

6 friends from your past you've got back in touch with because…
a) you want to make it clear to all the popular kids from school that you DID manage to get a husband in the end
b) you think they might now be in a position to give you work
c) you fancied them when you were about 16. Maybe they're still available
d) you'd heard they'd got divorced. Maybe their ex is available
e) you remember they had an older brother. Maybe their brother is still available
f) they had a cute French penpal who came to stay one summer and snogged you. Maybe they're still available
g) you thought a reunion with the old crowd would turn back the clock and make you all feel young again, though actually you all just drank far too much, said things you shouldn't and have been a mass of seething resentments ever since. Plus, you now feel even older

h) you saw them on a social networking site and decided to stalk them

i) you saw them on TV and decided to stalk them

j) you were on TV and want all the popular girls to know just how successful you are now

7 Friends you've always kept in touch with because…

a) If they ever told anyone about that time with you, Mickey thingy, the vodka and the fire extinguisher then it would not only be really embarrassing but bar you from certain professions on ethical grounds

b) You feel bad about the time you got off with their boyfriend behind their back when you were 15 (which in fact is okay because you still haven't twigged that at the same time they were getting off with yours. I mean, where did you think those love bites came from?)

c) They know your real age.

8 The one or two friends your partner has made to whom he actually remembered to introduce you

- -

MIDLIFE CONUNDRUM: **WHERE DID YOUR KNOWLEDGE GO**?

Just because you know that cappuccini is the plural of cappuccino, or shout at football commentators who incorrectly talk about Barcelona's Nou Camp (rhyming with shoe) instead of Camp Nou (rhyming with cow), doesn't mean you can speak a foreign language.

Maybe you *used to* be able to speak a foreign language. Maybe you au paired in Brussels, went InterRailing round Italy, or once bought a Spanish tape before a holiday. But don't let this fool you into thinking you can go into a bar in a foreign city and attempt to engage the natives in conversation.

What else have you forgotten since school? Differential calculus? Boyle's Law? The chemical symbol for silver? More than the first three lines of 'Four Quartets'? Why Ethelred was Unready? All this unused wisdom, which you spent your teens cramming into your eager brain, has been pushed aside in favour of:

1 an in-depth knowledge of a subject so specialised it's of absolutely no interest or use to anyone apart from other specialists – the regional sales figures for ink-jet printers in East Anglia; the top ten currently most competitive fixed-rate mortgages; primary school league tables in the Cheltenham area.

Which is complemented at the other end of the spectrum by...

2 a scattergun pub-quiz selection of random facts: the capital of Madagascar? Antananarivo! The date of the Battle of Bannockburn? 1314! The song that kept Ultravox's 'Vienna' from the Number One slot in 1981? Joe Dolce's 'Shaddap You Face'! The only London Tube station containing none of the letters of the word 'mackerel'? St John's Wood!

With very little actual information left in between.

Although you'd be hard pressed these days to pass any of the A levels you still confidently list on your CV, as long as you stick to pub banter and Trivial Pursuit, in your own mind you can still consider yourself an intellectual.

- -

TURNING INTO YOUR PARENTS

You will.

SKILLS YOU SHOULD POSSESS BY NOW

1 Changing a tyre
2 Filling in a tax return
3 Calming a screaming child at 3am in the A&E department of an overstretched local hospital
4 Contraception
5 Organising a funeral
6 Knowing how to use a semi-colon
7 Spontaneously crying in supermarkets at the sheer pain of being alive
8 Not panicking when someone asks you your name and you're briefly unable to tell them because YOU FORGOT
9 When, at Christmas, your ageing mother-in-law says, 'You don't want me here, I don't know why I bother coming,' resisting the urge to say, 'Shall I tell you why you bother? You bother because the few people you haven't alienated in your life by being horrible to them are dead and you have NOWHERE ELSE TO GO except your care home, so if you'd LIKE me to take you back there, JUST SAY THE WORD and I will get the car keys'
10 Relaxing

THINGS YOU <u>WILL</u> EVENTUALLY HEAR YOURSELF SAYING

'Of course, A levels were a lot harder when we took them.'

'Can you turn it down a notch?'

'I think these trousers must have shrunk.'

'I preferred the original version.'

'Everywhere looks the same these days.'

'You can't go out looking like that.'

'That's not a skirt, it's a top.'

'Tom Baker was the best Doctor Who.'

'Because I said so.'

'What's that noise?'

'Who would call at this hour?'

'Oh, no thanks, it'll keep me awake.'

'And to think we only had three channels.'

'You had a sort of spinning platform which you put the 'record' on and then you had to lift the tone arm and drop the stylus very carefully into the outlying groove...'

TRAUMATISED BY TELEVISION ALL OVER AGAIN

Is it any wonder we reach midlife so messed up when you consider some of the programmes we watched as children and teenagers – apparently innocent TV shows that were in fact much more disturbing than the self-evidently deranging computer games played by today's kids?

Until the advent of YouTube, much of this material was either lost or inaccessible to anyone who didn't work in a TV archive. This gave it the aura of a collective fever dream: *I must have seen it. It seemed so nightmarishly real at the time. But maybe I didn't. Maybe I'm going mad.*

It feels fascinatingly strange, to have lost a chunk of one's youth, only to get it back with interest later in life. But that, thanks to the internet, is the position we're in. And it's great when that youth includes Tom Baker's Doctor Who or Jenny Hanley on *'Magpie'*, less great when we're talking about, well, this sort of thing:

'Picture Box' (1967–88)

Granada-produced show for schools presented by corpse-faced one-time *Coronation Street* actor Alan Rothwell, who introduced film clips from around the world for the benefit of those children who hadn't been scared to within an inch of their lives by the opening credits showing a bejewelled, glass-sided, velvet-lined box rotating while swirly, atonal music ('Manege' by the French experimental composer Jacques Lasry) played in the background.

'Threads' (1984)

What would happen if a nuclear bomb fell on Sheffield? All kinds of bad stuff, though children allowed to stay up late to watch Barry Hines' impossibly bleak play would particularly remember the montage of animals writhing in agony, milk bottles melting and bodies frying as the Soviet Union dropped 210 megatons on the UK. No wonder you joined CND during your 'political phase' at university. Its director Mick Jackson would go on to make *The Bodyguard* with Whitney Houston. Thanks for that, Mick.

'Ask The Family' (1967–84, revived in 1999 and again, ironically, in 2005)

In its original, non-ironic incarnation, this was seemingly a competition to find the country's squarest families, broadcast from an eerie parallel universe where The Rolling Stones, punk and every other cultural revolution of the '60s and '70s never happened. Each team consisted of four family members – the parents and two terrifying Midwich Cuckoo teenage children. Robert Robinson presented version one, kids' TV stalwarts Dick and Dom the most recent (2005) revival. The show's creator, Patricia Owtram, was not impressed. 'I was disgusted,' she wrote in a letter of complaint, 'that in the first programme a boy who gave a wrong answer was forced to wear a donkey mask and be hooted.'

Noseybonk (notorious character from the BBC's mystery-word show 'Jigsaw' 1979–81)

By some distance the most distressing in a line-up that also included Jigg the sinister floating jigsaw piece and Pterry the sinister floating pterodactyl. Noseybonk, actually presenter Adrian Hedley, wore a tuxedo, white gloves and a white fright-mask with a huge distended nose which… which… I'm sorry, I can't go on.

OBSESSION WITH LISTS OF THINGS TO DO BEFORE YOU DIE

As if you weren't already busy enough, the stark realisation of your own mortality that characterises midlife triggers a blind panic about all the things you might never have time to do. To ensure you don't waste the rest of your life being distracted by the mundane or mediocre, you turn to lists of 'the 100 greatest...' [...novels you must read; ...albums to hear; ...birds to spot; ... Belgian beers to try, etc] and start making 'bucket' lists of essential things you now believe it's imperative to have experienced before you kick the proverbial.

Perhaps you see them as an insurance policy? 'I can't die yet! I still haven't visited Machu Picchu or played a round on the Old Course at St Andrews!' Or a get-out from life's everyday demands? 'I'm far too busy to do the washing up, I've still got *The Bicycle Thief* to watch and a crate of Lambic to drink if I want to keep on target.'

Better, surely, to enjoy life for the sake of it and relish the two or three great things you are doing, rather then the 98 or 97 you aren't? However exciting you think you can make your life, the mundane will always get you in the end. Sadly, the co-author of travel guide *100 Things To Do Before You Die*, Dave Freeman, died at just 47, having visited roughly half the places on his own list. His demise was not from being speared by a bull in Pamplona, or a freak ballooning accident, but from falling over at home and hitting his head.

Most common inclusions on 'bucket lists'

Test-drive a Ferrari
Read the best 100 novels/see the 100 best films
Take a trip in a hot-air balloon
Go to Wembley/Wimbledon
Have tea at the Ritz
Write a novel

Bet everything on red in a casino
See the Northern Lights
Visit the Seven Wonders of the World
Swim with dolphins
Apologise
Make a will

Most common entries on lists of things to do before you're 50
Skydive
Learn a language to a proficient standard
Learn to play the guitar
Grow a beard (men only)
Have nude photos taken
Go to ballet/opera
Lose weight
Run in a marathon/triathlon
Come out to your parents (rather than just assuming they must have
cottoned on by now)
Eat at a Michelin-starred restaurant

Make your own to do list

1 ....

2 ....

3 ....

4 ....

5 ....

6 ....

7 ....

8 ....

9 ....

10 ....

Evelyn Couch: Hey! I was waiting for that spot!
Girl 1: Face it, lady, we're younger and faster!
[Evelyn rear-ends the other car six times]
Girl 1: What are you *doing*?
Girl 2: Are you *crazy*?
Evelyn Couch: Face it, girls, I'm older and I have
more insurance.

'Fried Green Tomatoes at the Whistle Stop Café' (1991)

MIDLIFE HEROINE:

Debbie Harry

Debbie Harry was already in her mid-thirties when Blondie were enjoying their imperial phase in the late 1970s and early '80s: 33 when their album Parallel Lines *went to Number One; 36 when she released her first solo album,* Koo-Koo; *49 when she teamed up with New York avant-garde ensemble The Jazz Passengers; and 53 when* 'Maria' *by the reformed Blondie topped the singles charts.*

THINGS TO LOOK FORWARD TO WHEN YOU GET EVEN OLDER

1 Free bus travel (having had years to work out which bus routes go where)
2 Comfortable footwear (especially those really cosy-looking fur-lined booties with zips)
3 Shopping bags on wheels
4 Carte blanche to be rude to people
5 Carte blanche to hold forth at length on any subject, with the assumption that you are right just because you are older than everyone else
6 Pretending you can't remember something when really you just can't be bothered to think about it
7 Conveniently selective hearing
8 Knowing what you like and refusing to apologise for it
9 Tins of travel sweets
10 In a hostage situation, you will be among the first to be released
11 Getting younger people to do all your shopping for you
12 Finally shaking off all the friends you made in Freshers' Week
13 No one expecting you to run anywhere
14 HRT
15 Cats. Lots of cats
16 Finally being able to get a job in a charity shop
17 Wearing mismatched clothes
18 Those little golf buggies old or obese people are allowed to drive down crowded pavements
19 Playing tricks on your grandchildren by sitting very, very still and pretending you're not breathing
20 Making up stuff about the past because no one else was born then
21 Taking up smoking. What are people going to say? It might kill you?

MIDLIFE DILEMMA: 'I'M STILL NOT SURE WHAT I WANT TO BE WHEN I GROW UP'

You spend most of your twenties in denial about being a 'grown-up', waiting for the enlightenment you think happens when you finally reach 'adulthood' – a mystical state where the world makes sense, relationships are finally straightforward, you know who you are and your ambitions become clear.

In fact, enlightenment comes with the blinding realisation that this is as mature as you're going to get: the older generations you looked up to (your parents) don't have a clue either and have basically been winging it all these years.

The state of confusion in which you exist is, we must tell you, permanent. If you think you are a late developer because you don't yet know what to do with your life, that's normal. No one does. Why do you think all your friends are suddenly quitting their jobs?

If anything, your self-knowledge and general understanding of life, the universe and everything probably peaked in your early thirties. From here on, it's a gradual descent into confusion and befuddlement. Sorry.

- -

'A man is only as old as the woman he feels.'

Groucho Marx

- -

OTHER THINGS BESIDES YOU THAT ARE OVER 40

Mainframe computers (1964)

Felt tips (1962)

Hypertext (1965)

Barbie (1959)

Microchips (1959)

Sesame Street (1969)

Time Out magazine (1968)

Miniskirts (1965)

Mr Potato Head (1952)

Hovercraft (1956)

The Hula Hoop (1958)

CDs (1965)

ATMs (1969)

2.
GROOMING

Just as you'd finally come to terms with what you look like, everything starts to change. Some bits of you have an unwanted growth spurt (waist, pecs, *ears!*), while other bits shrink (cheeks, lips, ability to judge what it is appropriate for a person of your age to wear). Hair starts growing everywhere *except* your head. On the one hand your tattoos are becoming increasingly hard to carry off; on the plus side you can finally start wearing slippers.

THE UNPARALLELED HORROR OF ENCOUNTERING YOUR OWN REFLECTION FIRST THING IN THE MORNING

Arrghhhh! Who's that pale spectre in the mirror? The one with the blood-drained lips, pallid skin and dead eyes? It looks like you, but with the colour and brightness turned down: a chilling vision of yourself as a cadaver. Not so long ago you had distinct features – red lips, blue eyes, brown eyebrows, vaguely consistent skin. But now – now you're a pixellated blur of uneven tones, red blotches, grey-green shadows and blue lines. Even your neighbours fail to recognise you before you've evened out your pigmentation and drawn your personality back on. You may not have been a make-up counter groupie in the past, but these days you daren't pop out for a paper without a touch of tinted moisturiser and a dab of mascara lest some helpful soul worries that you are near death and calls a paramedic.

- -

THE BIG FIVE MIDLIFE GROOMING MUST-DOS

Dyeing

It seeps from the temples and springs from the parting. And dye as you might, there's no escaping the fact that you have GREY HAIR.

Of course, if you are a man, you can play the Silver Fox card and women will swoon – at least, they did in films in the 1970s. Men do occasionally give in to the temptation to dye – see Paul McCartney, who has been dyeing since the mid-1980s, save for a brief appearance in 1986 on *The Tube* in which he attempts to carry off the Silver Fox look while performing a song called 'Only Love Remains'. (Take a look on YouTube. Better or worse? Or just a bit washed out and not like the Paul McCartney you know and love?)

But if you do decide to dye, remember male hair doesn't take the colour very well, and as it thins the effect becomes even more ridiculous and unconvincing. To look halfway decent, you need to do what women do and go professional. And that will cost you.

Sadly for women, no one's invented the Silver Vixen yet. Unless you're going to a *Josie and the Pussycats* themed party as Alexandra Cabot or secretly want to be Rogue from *X Men*, the advantages of being a grey-haired woman are few. The good news is that greying is genetically predetermined – ie you really can blame your parents for this one.

Plucking

How did hair get THERE? I mean, that's not a part of the body that's supposed to have hair on it. I've spent decades waxing, threading and depilating, pulling hairs out of intimate areas by their roots, and now you want me to start plucking THERE as well? How are there even hair follicles THERE? And why are some of the hairs grey already?

Concealing

The Georgians used white lead paint to create a fashionably even complexion. The Victorian middle classes drank vinegar and painted blue veins on their skin to keep pale and prove they were too grand to have been working outside. That's when they weren't dilating their pupils and flushing their cheeks with belladonna. Luckily, you can probably find something more convincing and less toxic at Boots.

Face it – broken veins, *rosacea*, dark circles under your eyes, blotchiness and the general appearance of being knackered are with you for the duration. If this is not the look you are going for, then foundations, concealers, powders, green creams (hide redness) and tinted moisturisers can be applied with increasing thickness to give the illusion that your complexion is as natural as your hair colour.

And men, we know you do it too. We've seen the concealer stick hidden behind the tough-looking shaving products – it's next to the man exfoliator and the hand cream.

Plumping & moisturising

When did my skin change from being, well, skin-like to having the texture and thickness of cellophane? I'm sure when I used to move a bit of it, it eventually moved back to where it was before, instead of just staying there in that flappy, ghostly way.

What? You've got a special cream containing lots of something called retinol that's guaranteed to get some of the collogen/elasticity back? And another to plump up my 'sensitive eye area'? And one for my lips? And one for my neck? And one for my décolletage? And a funny roll-on stick I can trail around my face so I can fool myself that I'm targeting wrinkles? Great! Sorry, it costs *how* much? For a moisturiser? That's just a tax on ageing.

And it's not just collagen you're low on these days. Sebaceous glands produce less oil as you age so your skin will become dry and itchy, especially during the winter months. You could pay through the nose for posh moisturisers – or you could just get a big tub of super-cheap aqueous cream, which will have the same effect.

Flossing

The only people who floss regularly before the age of 35 are Americans and those with hardcore orthodontic conditions. For everyone else, it's just an irksome staple of that awkward end-of-session conversation you have with your dentist, assuming you visit a dentist, which maybe you don't because Christ knows they're expensive these days if you can't find an NHS one.

During midlife, however, flossing starts to matter. Or rather, the fact that you haven't flossed until now starts to matter because your teeth are fucked. Look at them: scaly, yellow, misshapen, fang-like things. Aren't you ashamed? Of course you are. It's why you tried bleaching them with one of those kits. It's why you no longer smile properly in photographs. It's why you're always breathing into your cupped palm to check if your breath smells.

You should floss your teeth at least once a day. You shouldn't need us to tell you that the point of flossing is to remove food debris and plaque from in between the teeth that a toothbrush can't reach. But maybe you do. Maybe you were too busy writing 'John Taylor is lush' on your pencil case to pay attention during science. Anyway, plaque is a film of bacteria that causes tooth decay and can lead to gum disease. The first stage of gum disease is gingivitis – swelling or infection of the gums. The second stage is periodontal disease, where the bone anchoring your teeth in your mouth rots away. Periodontal disease is horrible and expensive to treat, so look: floss, okay? Also, stop smoking and try to manage your alcohol intake.

Oh yes: flossing could also prevent you from having a stroke or heart attack, according to a study published in the February 8, 2005 edition of *Circulation* magazine – it exists, honestly – which found a strong link between gum disease and narrowing of the arteries (atherosclerosis). So that's good.

TATTOOS AND PIERCINGS

By this stage, either you've got a tattoo or you haven't. Either way, there's no going back.

If you jumped on the bandwagon in your clubbing days, you may now be regretting having to wear long sleeves all summer so that your business clients don't see the Celtic tribal design that weaves up your lower arm. Or finding it almost impossible to match smart spiky heels with the strawberry on your ankle.

If, however, you were too sensible (or scared of pain) to get tattooed and/ or pierced before your thirties, you probably envy those friends who can flash their cheeky little navel ring as a badge of a well-spent misspent youth. 'Look at me,' it shouts, 'I was *interesting*.'

You may even find yourself thinking, 'It's not too late. Maybe, I could just get a little bluebird done above my jeans waistband. Hardly anyone would even know it was there. What would be the harm?'

Now picture yourself actually going into a tattoo parlour, one full of young, cool people and people much harder than you. And then exposing your wrinkled, dimpled love handles to the tattoo artist. Then having to admit to your partner and children what you've done.

'Shame' doesn't even cover it.

WHAT NOT TO WEAR FROM YOUR FORTIES ONWARDS...

Men:
Bandanas
Glasses where the brand name is bigger than the pupil of your eye
Snake belts
Anything fluorescent/day-glo
Ties with repetitive patterns of small animals
Power Rangers costumes (Superman is fine)
Snoods
Your lunch
Baseball caps
Jeans lower than the waistband of your Y-fronts
Nylon replica football tops, especially when they're a size too small –
invest in a Paul Smith football T-shirt instead
Badges
Your old university scarf – it was 25 years ago, for God's sake
Heelies (or ride children's scooters)

Women:
Anything too short without the modesty of at least 40 denier tights,
especially at parents' evening
Boob tubes
Legwarmers – unless you are actually a professional dancer
Things that have come back into fashion from when you were 14: it isn't
about whether it suits you, it's the psychological trauma that concerns us
Underwear as outerwear, however many times that one comes back into
fashion
Fairy wings, devil's horns, deely boppers, etc, even on a hen night, even
on your daughter's hen night, or your mother's
Roller boots, unless at a designated roller-skating arena and accompanied
by children as an excuse
Bold patterns – they may get confused with your varicose veins

Head-to-toe Boden: do mix and match with other brands
The same outfit as your mother – really, it's not compulsory
The same outfit as your daughter – really, when people asked if you were sisters *they were being ironic*

SLIPPERS

In your twenties you thought slippers were embarrassing. For old people, or very young people, or damaged sociopaths like that evangelical Christian girl who lived on your corridor at university. Her giant fluffy slippers had pigs' faces on them. You and your nasty friends made fun of them and said they were a cry for help. 'Freudian slippers' – yes, that was what you called them. But secretly you thought: *I bet they're really cosy. When she's working late at night and it's cold, I bet those slippers really hit the spot.*

Because you were in slipper denial you wore flip-flops, sandals and other types of lightweight indoor footwear. You believed this was the modern, cosmopolitan way forward.

One day, a friend brought you back from Japan a pair of those special slippers the Japanese wear to prevent 'clean' areas like kitchens from being contaminated by 'dirty' areas like toilets. They were made of green rubber, which amused you. 'Kinky' – yes, that was the word you used. You wore them for a bit, ironically. And of course they were useless, not like proper slippers at all. They were cold and drafty and made an annoying flapping noise when you walked. You threw them away.

To celebrate your 38th birthday, you and your then-boyfriend, now your best friend's husband, went to Lynmouth in north Devon. You stayed in a B&B a short walk from the harbour. You argued about where to eat and whether it was exhibitionist to have sex when you knew other people could hear you. (You claimed it was. Your then-boyfriend recognised this immediately as an exit strategy.) On the morning of the day you were due to leave, you went for a walk by yourself and found a boutique specialising in leather and sheepskin goods. In a wicker basket by the door was an assortment of sheepskin slippers with furry white lining and Cornish pasty-style crenellations around the lateral edge.

You picked up a pair and held them in the palm of your hand, as if weighing them. Then you took them inside to where a leather-jacketed woman with badly hennaed hair sat behind the counter listening to Radio 2 and bought them using your Visa card. They cost £15, which you thought was a bit steep.

You have never looked back.

MIDLIFE HERO:

Richard Briers in *Ever Decreasing Circles*

Everyone remembers Briers as Tom Good in The Good Life, *and that's as it should be. But he was equally brilliant in* Ever Decreasing Circles, *which boasted the same writers (John Esmonde and Bob Larbey) and ran from 1984-89. Like* The Good Life, *its focus was the midlife suburban predicament – but the tone was darker as obsessive organiser Martin (Briers' character) became locked in almost murderous rivalry with laid-back neighbour Paul (Peter Egan).*

women

MAKING AN EFFORT

One of the many unpalatable midlife epiphanies for women is that one has to start Making An Effort. Unbrushed hair, bitten nails and holes in the armpits of your cardigan can be sexy in your twenties, in an Iris Murdoch, mind-on-higher-matters kind of way. In your thirties, the same things will make you look a mess. In your forties, you will just look like a mad old bat.

Contrary to what women's magazines would have us believe, grooming is tedious, life-denying, and at times morally thorny. It means buying products such as lint removers from hitherto unvisited sections of John Lewis, spending a morning a month you will never get back having your roots done, and feeling uncomfortable as a silent Filipino woman crouches at your feet scouring your cracked heels.

You begin to live in fear of a light drizzle, which can seriously ruin your hairdo; in the summer you are forced to coordinate your social life around fake tan applications.

And the result of this never-ending palaver? Not, as you would expect from so much effort, a rare beauty who will hush a room upon entering. All this is just basic upkeep, taming your vile, unruly body to the degree where it doesn't actually give offence.

THE LANGUAGE OF AGEING

Long ago, when you first started buying face creams, the sell itself was alluring. Manufacturers woo the young with adjectives like *kind, soothing, nourishing, purifying, protecting, balancing, refreshing*. They promise natural radiance with things they label not plain old 'moisturiser' but 'beauty fluid', 'Youth Code' (implying youth is a secret forbidden to us oldies) and 'Cashmere Moments'. To use such a cream is to belong to a club of dewy-skinned under-thirties; to inhabit a land where it is forever spring.

But as the summer of your life draws in, the language on the pots changes to fighting talk. Creams shout about their 'targeted zone action'; they *fight* existing lines, *resist* age, *defy* time, they are *anti*-wrinkle and anti-ageing (as opposed to being *pro*-youth). They roll out the science, knowing it's so long since you did your A Levels that you're clueless enough to believe anything. They start dropping in buzz-words like pro-retinol (basically vitamin A), pro-xylane (a sugar-protein hybrid chemically engineered to promote firmer skin), AHAs (alpha hydroxy acids such as lactic acid, found in sour milk and unripe apples) and talk about a science called *aqua physics*.

The sheer magnitude of the task in hand is conveyed by names such as *ultra* lift. There's sci-fi talk of *regeneration* and *dermagenesis* and Moisture *Miracle*, a nod to the impossibility of the situation.

Dare to age past 50 and the urgency becomes even greater. 'Vital' is shouted from creams for the over 50s – vital as in the basis of life, yes, but also as in 'if you don't do this you'll only have yourself to blame for being cast out from society'. In this arena, creams call themselves things like Wrinkle De-Crease, as if your face is a stubborn piece of laundry, while the number of *restoration* creams, *strippers* and *fillers* around makes you feel even more like an old ruin.

TOPSHOP

While it's perfectly acceptable these days for grown-ups to shop in high street chains originally invented for teenagers (Topshop, Topman, River Island, New Look, Gap, etc), there are, nevertheless, rules:

• Don't think you can fit into a size 12 in one of these places if that's the size you normally take in Marks & Spencer.
• Anything labelled as a 'dress' will probably be the length of what you know as a 'top' and should therefore be worn accordingly.
• 'Tops', by extension, are designed to skim the bottom of your rib cage. This may not be the midriff-displaying look you are going for.
• If you can't work out which way round you're supposed to wear it, it is probably too fashionable for you.
• Only try on shoes wide enough to accommodate your bunions.
• On no account frequent any in-house nail bars, juice bars, hair salons, or tattoo parlours. These genuinely are for younger clientele only.
• Do not buy anything decorated with love hearts, bows, Hello Kitty, Bob Marley, or slogans. Even ironically.

- -

WOULD YOU INJECT YOUR FACE WITH BABY FORESKIN?

If you have enough cash and a strong stomach, there's no end to the lengths you can go in your quest for eternal youth. Among the options we've uncovered are:

• tiny skin cells called fibroblasts derived from the foreskins of circumcised babies, suspended in a clear liquid. Used for treating scarring, from burns to acne, as well as removal of lines round mouth. www.vavelta.com;
• anti-ageing serums based on viper venom to paralyse your facial muscles;

- facial fillers derived from cock's combs (aka Restylane);
- botox, of course, or rather Botulinum toxin type A, essentially a poison which inhibits your neurotransmitters (the chemicals that transmit messages through your muscles, ie it paralyses them;
- collagen marshmallows and collagen-infused mineral water (both available in Japan);
- growing your own breast implants from your own fat and stem cells (devised in Japan);
- nightingale poo face wash (Japan again – they are obsessed with anti-ageing treatments, apparently);
- stretchmark creams now marketed for the face. And piles creams now marketed for eye bags;
- acids that burn the top layer of skin off your face. On purpose;
- gore-tex lip implants (the stuff they make waterproof hiking jackets out of).

Undoubtedly, you will look younger than your years once you've endured treatments like these. But is it really your years you want to look younger than, or your peers?

If everyone is on Botox/Restylane/baby foreskin, then everyone is going to look younger. Which means 35-year-olds will look 28, 40-year-olds 34, 50-year-olds 38, etc. In other words, everyone is back to looking their age, because that's what their age now looks like.

Men

MALE PATTERN BALDNESS – ALOPECIA ANDROGENETICA

According to the NHS, male pattern baldness affects 6.5 million men in the UK and usually develops in your thirties (though it can start in your late teens). It's most prevalent among Caucasians and Afro-Caribbeans, rare in Japan, and unheard of among Native Americans.

It's caused by dihydrotestosterone (DHT), produced by the male hormone testosterone, which makes the hair follicles shrink and eventually stop functioning. However, the fact that it's brought on by testosterone does NOT mean you can claim to be more virile just because you're bald.

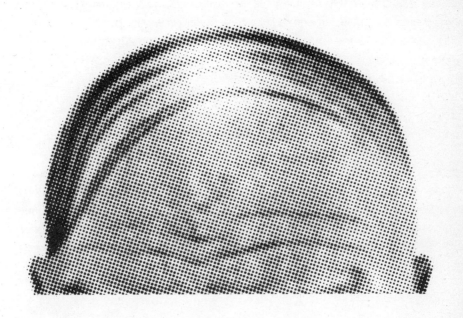

There are lots of 'cures' on the market:

- Hormone tablets (finasteride)
- Ointments to rub into your head (minoxidil)
- Skin grafts from hairier areas of your body (eew!)
- Hair implants from 'donors'
- Weaves
- Wigs

But why bother? Much easier to conspire with your fellow afflicted and make MPB a fashion statement. Shave off the rest, team it with a close-fitting John Smedley jumper and some dark wash-jeans and hey presto, you're Media Dad! Or combine it with serious spectacles for that Architect/French Philosopher look. Norman Foster, Michael Stipe, Vin Diesel, and, er, Bruce Willis – we salute you.

But why stop there? Why not exploit the commercial opportunities? With every other inch of our environment now covered with promotional imagery, sell this unadulterated acreage for advertising space. Or get an Arts Council grant and let Banksy loose.

'OLD MAN' EARS

As men get older, their ears get bigger. Women's ears get bigger too, but you don't notice so much because their ears are smaller to start with. Your ears grow throughout life because they're made of cartilage, which continues to grow as you age – unlike bone, which normally stops growing soon after puberty. Did you know that the external flappy bit of your ear is called the pinna? Well, you do now.

NASAL AND EAR HAIR

Nasal hair is one of the more repulsive manifestations of male ageing. It's always been there, of course, but its growth escalates after 30 so that soon spiky strands of the stuff are protruding from your nostrils. Sometimes, when you blow your nose, snot gets caught on it. But you don't realise this, so you walk around oblivious to your resemblance to Mr Twit in *The Twits*, making innocent conversation with all sorts of people, some of them attractive, and all the while these globules are vibrating and threatening to detach themselves.
You need to trim. Not pluck – plucking is bad because the root can get infected. Trim with scissors, or with one of those fancy electric trimmers which has a spinning blade. (You can use them on your eyebrows too, not to mention your ear hair – yes, that's right, ear hair.) Remember that nasal hair is there for a reason: to filter out rubbish, including germs, before you inhale it. You're not supposed to get rid of it entirely.

Ear hair, incidentally, is mostly a post-midlife phenomenon. Not everyone gets it either – it's thought to be an inherited trait, passed along on the father's side through the Y chromosome. An American survey in the mid-1980s found that 74% of men had ear hair. But that sounds excessive to us.

- -

DISGUISING YOUR PAUNCH

Men store their excess weight in front of their abdomens. In a bid to distract you from this, they employ a variety of cunning camouflage measures. (All right, not a variety – just the one. This one: not tucking in their shirts. Had you fooled, though, didn't it?) Wearing dark colours helps, too. Also: not pulling a belt so tight that your gut spills out over the top.

The last resort for the man who is both out of shape and exceptionally vain is a slimming girdle, which – just to set the record straight – William Shatner *didn't* wear while filming *Star Trek*. It's a myth, he says, Okay? Girdles are basically huge rubber bands that you pull around your waist and fasten with hooks. They cover everything from the base of your pecs to your hip bone. But we'll say this again because the truth is always worth reiterating: William Shatner *didn't wear one*. Ever. It was a bandage after he broke a rib riding a horse.

MOOBS

They're not necessarily a result of obesity, you know. And they've worked well for Jack Nicholson over the years. Still, chances are you don't like yours much. They wouldn't be so bad if they weren't so… hairy.

There are a number of ways to combat moobs:

- Wear a loose-fitting shirt.
- Never go anywhere where you might feel you have to take this shirt off, eg a beach.
- Do some exercise – that sometimes helps.
- Spend £4,000 having them surgically removed.
- Er, that's it.

CARDIGANS

Men's cardigans enjoyed a renaissance in the early 1990s when they were an essential indie-kid accessory, perfect for wearing over Ride or My Bloody Valentine T-shirts. The point was shabbiness rather than chic. If yours was flecked with spag bog or you'd burnt a hole in the arm after falling asleep with a joint between your fingers, then so much the better.

The garment's alleged inventor was James Thomas Brudenell, the 7th Earl of Cardigan, who led the Charge of the Light Brigade during the Crimean War. In 1855, thanks to his relentless boasting and exaggeration of his role in the exercise, he stepped ashore back in England to find himself a celebrity and clothes shops doing a roaring trade in replicas of the 'knitted waistcoat' he wore on campaign.

Later, they became popular with fishermen. So they have quite a macho lineage really, if you're insecure enough to care about that kind of thing.

The advantages of cardigans over pullovers are numerous:

• The buttons mean you're less likely to injure yourself taking them off than with jumpers, where the pulling-over-head manoeuvre has been known to result in sprains and dislocations.
• You can always unbutton or unzip a cardigan to improve air flow around your torso – not so with a jumper
• The 'moob' factor (see Moobs) makes it impossible for most men over 40 to wear polo necks, tight-fitting John Smedley jumpers, etc. Cardigans are much more flattering.

3.
HAPPY FAMILIES

You always knew the 'nuclear family' was a convenient fiction. Even so, nothing can prepare you for the brain-scrambling complexity of the midlife ménage. There you are, sandwiched between ageing parents and petulant children, and with a family tree so messy it would floor a team of researchers from *Who Do You Think You Are?*

THE FAMILY TREE OF THE AVERAGE MIDLIFER

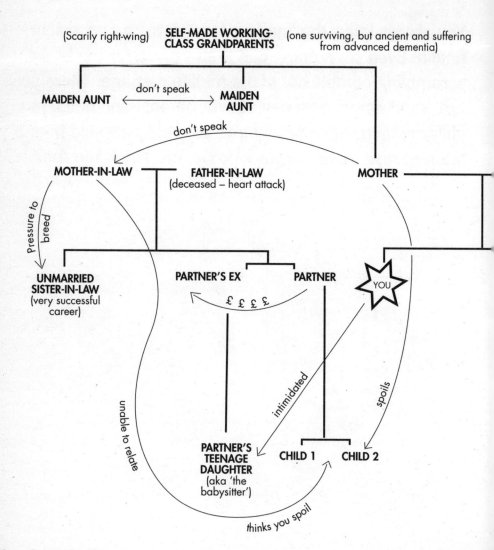

(Scarily right-wing) **SELF-MADE WORKING-CLASS GRANDPARENTS** (one surviving, but ancient and suffering from advanced dementia)

MAIDEN AUNT ← don't speak → **MAIDEN AUNT**

don't speak

MOTHER-IN-LAW   **FATHER-IN-LAW** (deceased – heart attack)   **MOTHER**

Pressure to breed

UNMARRIED SISTER-IN-LAW (very successful career)

PARTNER'S EX   **PARTNER**   **YOU**

£ £ £ £

unable to relate

intimidated

spoils

PARTNER'S TEENAGE DAUGHTER (aka 'the babysitter')   **CHILD 1**   **CHILD 2**

thinks you spoil

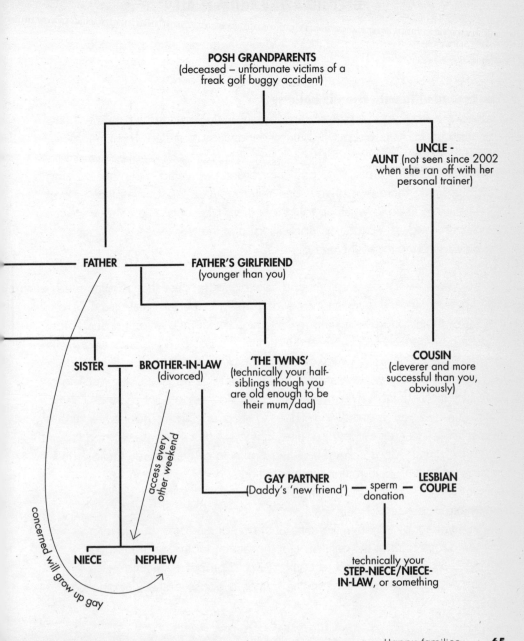

POSH GRANDPARENTS
(deceased – unfortunate victims of a
freak golf buggy accident)

UNCLE -
AUNT (not seen since 2002
when she ran off with her
personal trainer)

FATHER ——— **FATHER'S GIRLFRIEND**
(younger than you)

COUSIN
(cleverer and more
successful than you,
obviously)

SISTER ——— **BROTHER-IN-LAW**
(divorced)

'THE TWINS'
(technically your half-
siblings though you
are old enough to be
their mum/dad)

access every
other weekend

GAY PARTNER
(Daddy's 'new friend') — sperm
donation

LESBIAN
COUPLE

concerned will grow up gay

NIECE   **NEPHEW**

technically your
STEP-NIECE/NIECE-
IN-LAW, or something

GETTING AWAY FROM IT ALL

Travel broadens the mind and that's a lovely thing. But what if it also shortens your life?

The rented-villa-with-friends holiday

A hangover from your 20-something days. What if you tried it again with the same(ish) group of people? Ah, but the dynamic has altered! Last time, all your differences were kept in check thanks to a shared assumption that the point of the holiday was, in no particular order, swimming, sleeping, drinking and shagging. There was always one self-appointed tour guide or fretter over hygiene ('We need to wash up tonight or there'll be ants!'), but they were easily dismissed as 'uptight' or 'controlling' and the pack worked as one to exclude them and make them cry.

Ten years on, *everyone* is uptight and controlling because they're exhausted and have so much invested in the holiday being a success. Debates rumble like the thunderstorm which kicks in on Day 3 (leading to enforced and furious watching of the only DVD you can find in the house: *Bridget Jones' Diary* with Italian subtitles you can't switch off). Should younger children be allowed to stay up late, Mediterranean style? Why is X passively-aggressively insisting on doing all the cooking? What can you say or do to stop Y's 12-year-old son from staring at your breasts? Why does Z keep leaving the pool cover off? And why, just because a few people want to go off by themselves and look at a nearby church, does A keep referring darkly to a 'breakaway faction' and sighing whenever their names are mentioned?

Camping

On the one hand, you love the idea of the great outdoors, that *Swallows and Amazons* spirit of adventure: sleeping out under the stars – just you, the elements, a canvas sheet, a camp stove, a proper coffee-maker, free-range bacon bought straight from the farmer, a goose-feather sleeping bag, somewhere to charge your laptop... On the other, you are so conditioned for office work that you've no idea what to do with a mallet, other than perhaps tenderise steak or, at a pinch, play croquet.

The last time you went camping, you were ten. Your parents chucked – insofar as its heaviness permitted such an action – an antique A-frame tent into the back of the Morris Minor and sat you and your sister on top. (Seatbelts? What seatbelts?) You've never been tempted since... until now. Because now, well, everyone's doing it. Here's the deal: you'll give it a go if you can do it comfortably (Airstream trailer, gypsy caravan, yurt) and with loads of gadgets (self-heating food pouches, self-inflating mattresses, hand-held GPS systems, portable hot showers, portable refrigerators, portable toilets). Actually, you read something the other day about a campsite in France where you can stay in a luxury safari tent and sleep in a four-poster bed. Maybe that's worth looking into?

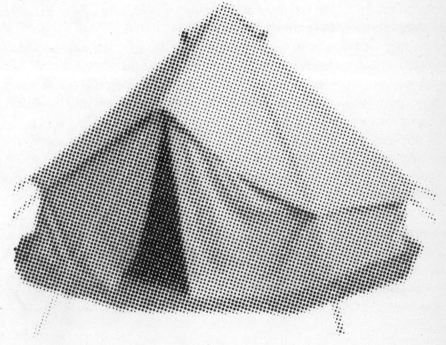

The sod-it-let's-go-to-Center Parcs holiday

You're supposed to be going camping, but the weather is foul, foul, foul. You swore you'd never go to Center Parcs. 'Over my dead body' – yes, that's what you said. But when you told the kids that camping was off they stopped talking to you, preferring to communicate via hurt, reproachful glances. So you took a deep breath, went online and... Christ, look at it – look at the 'subtropical swimming paradise' and Aqua Sana spa ('a sensuous journey of spa sensations') and Café *sodding* Rouge. No, no – stop being negative. Concentrate. Okay: do you want a three-bedroom Woodland Lodge or a Comfort Villa? (Which one's cheaper?) Will the children want to go windsurfing or paintballing or trek through the forest? Actually, at the risk of sounding like a press release, there's no shortage of activities. Maybe it isn't *such* a bad idea. The whole dome thing is fascinatingly creepy, and there's a good chance you'll get *Wolf Hall* finished if the kids are off riding giraffes or making weapons out of sticks.

The exhaust-the-grandparents holiday

Granny and Grandpa have retired to Somerset. Lucky Granny and Grandpa! And lucky you, because when half-term approaches you can get straight on the phone. 'You don't fancy having Jason for a week, do you? He's no trouble. He's got his iPhone and DS so he'll happily sit in his room playing by himself. *By* himself, not *wi*... No, quite.' Alternatively, you can *all* pile into the car. The kids can sleep on mattresses on the floor. Your parents won't mind giving up their bed for you: they understand how hard you work, much harder – you like to remind them – than they ever worked. (Your father left school at 16 and worked in a tin tray factory in Shepherd's Bush. He's dined out on this for years but the truth is he didn't actually have to *do* very much: it was just glorified standing around.) Idea: what if Granny and Grandpa move out for a few days into that Travelodge near Bridgwater? It's very quiet considering it's on the M5.

The claustrophobic hotel holiday

You wanted a quick, cheapish hit of winter sun. So here you are in... well, it's

Sharm El Sheikh, but it could be anywhere. Could be Dubai. Could be Leeds. Okay, not Leeds – Watford. If Watford was really, really hot. The hotel is clean and smart in a generic 5-star-hotel sort of way. The staff are friendly and helpful to the point where you start expecting them to confide in you about their self-evidently inhumane working conditions: 'My boss – he beat me for being late', 'Once I work 48 straight hours without sleep', etc. There's lots for the kids to do if you can be bothered to negotiate the pre-booking system. About 17 different pools. Lots of sports. 'Entertainment' in a conference room with a mic-stand at the far end: on Tuesday nights Ahmed the main pool attendant sings a song about a camel. Talking of camels, the Sinai By Moonlight tour to the fake Bedouin tent was a bit of a fiasco. The one you rode on had an open wound on its side. (You say 'rode' – the poor thing could barely stand up.) Christ, it's hot. 47 degrees. You never thought you'd be dreaming of snow.

The trip of a lifetime with an elderly relative you're worried might die soon

Your aunt saw it advertised in the back of the *Telegraph* – 'see the ancient sights of Syria' – and has guilt-tripped you into chaperoning her, possibly by paying for you, seeing as you still don't seem to have a proper job or be earning what you should. You envisaged something like Agatha Christie's *Murder in Mesopotamia* and hoped you might meet a dashing archaeologist in a neatly pressed safari suit. But what you've actually ended up with is a coachload of OAPs flirting with each other and a nine-day running commentary on how your dad always got all the attention because he was the youngest. While you wilt in the desert heat, your elderly relative, supposedly at death's door, strides through wadis and around mosques getting very excited about things even older than she is. Before long, one ancient ruin has started to look pretty much like another. And the next time you see this much sand you want it to be on a beach.

FAMILY ARGUMENTS

A recent survey of 3,000 familes found that the average family has at least three disagreements a day, each lasting up to five minutes. (The key phrase here, surely, is 'at least'.) Among the topics most likely to spark rows are:

- money, everyone's lack of (compounded by children pinching it from your purse whenever you're not looking)
- chores
- mislaying of vital equipment, eg remote control
- mouldy pizza under teenage beds
- the why we can't get a dog question
- treating this house like a hotel
- lack of domestic involvement by, and general uselessness of, father figure

It is possible to avoid most of the above scenarios by hiring a housekeeper, wearing earplugs, putting the remote on string like your mum used to do with your mittens, *actually* living in a hotel and not having kids.

Far easier just to admit defeat, pour yourself a large glass of wine and ignore everyone else in your household.

'What most persons consider as virtue, after the age of forty is simply a loss of energy.'

Voltaire

MIDLIFE CONUNDRUM: **HOW CAN I GET MY CHILD INTO THE BEST NOT-EXACTLY-LOCAL SCHOOL WITHOUT LOSING WHAT LITTLE INTEGRITY I STILL HAVE AND GENERALLY BECOMING A 'SCHOOLS BORE'?**

The short answer is... er.. you can't. Getting your child into the school of your choice is the closest the middle classes get to mortal combat, and consequently only the toughest survive. So ditch those socialist ideals of your youth and stop that namby-pamby squealing about ethics. Here's how to make the system work for you:

1 Start going to church – religious schools perform on average better than community schools. Or pay for your local church to get a new roof then emotionally blackmail the vicar.

2 Rent a place as near as possible to the school for the requisite vetting period. Where necessary, concoct fanciful stories about splitting up with your partner, then realising it was all a mistake and getting back together the minute the offer of a school place comes through.

3 Seduce a parent with a child already at your target school – the 'sibling rule' applies to step-siblings as well as actual siblings, and formal marriage is not required. Again, you can always split up later.

4 Make your child learn the bassoon. Many secondary schools reserve a certain percentage of places for music scholars. But go for instruments of a low register (really, you don't want to be in a house with a nine-year-old practising for their Grade 1 violin, and if they must repeat 'Greensleeves' ad nauseam on the recorder, make sure it's a tenor not a descant).

5 Start your own school. Or buy one of these newfangled 'academies'. Then you can force everyone to learn Latin, like you had to.

DEALING WITH OTHER PEOPLE'S CHILDREN

Even if you don't have any of these particular accessories yourself, by now you will almost certainly know someone who does. And they will almost certainly inflict them on you at some point, whether you ask them to or not. And you will almost certainly be expected to enjoy it.

Here are a few pointers to steer you through this most trying of situations:

Even though all babies look the same, do not get their names wrong. Or their gender

Do remember to compliment their parents on how articulate/ knowledgable/ talented their children are. If they patently aren't, just remark on how much they've grown

Do not try to be their 'mate'. It makes you look even older and more pathetic than they already thought you were

Do not give them your iPhone to play with. It will keep them still and quiet, yes, but you may find that your ring tone has been changed to a recording of them swearing and giggling

Do not resort to physical violence – unless their parents aren't looking

Do use alcohol as an anaesthetic for your nerves

Do not throw food, even if they started it

MIDLIFE CONUNDRUM: **WORKING PARENT GUILT**

'I mean, I like spending time with you, Mum. It would be good if you could get a job.'

Great. You spend your working life feeling guilty that you aren't spending enough time with your children. You give up your job to rectify this seemingly basic error. And it turns out they're not even that bothered. They'd rather have the extra cash.

Beyond age nine, you're lucky if they let you pick them up from school; then before you know it, they've cut their own door key and talked you into getting them a mobile phone. You are now only required for handing out cash, getting things from high shelves and knowing where everyone's stuff is when they think they've lost it.

Kids are brilliant company – as insightful, witty and entertaining as any adult. But let's face it, home life is mostly about dull practicality and routine-enforcement, from dragging everyone out of bed in the morning to forcing them back in again at night, with a reasonable amount of yelling in between. Being around each other 24/7 is boring. Even your kids think so.

'Middle age is when you're sitting at home on a Saturday night and the telephone rings and you hope it isn't for you.'

Ogden Nash

MOVING TO THE COUNTRY – WITH TEENAGERS

You talked about it when the kids were small, and they loved the idea of having trees to climb, woods to build dens in, beaches to explore or cute farm animals to name. Only you could never quite bring yourself to sacrifice your city life... until now.

So you assemble your kids, now all in double figures, and tell them the great news. Hey kids, we've found a house and we're all going to move to the countryside!

But strangely they aren't impressed. In fact, they're furious. Their friends! Their band! Their dealer!

However, they are still legally too young to live on their own and so for the last couple of years that you can, you are going to make the most of being the boss.

Instead of spending their teens in Manchester clubs they sulk them out in a picturesque fishing village in Fife where they refuse to make any friends because a) they are way too cool to talk to provincial types who just wouldn't 'get' them; b) they have no intention of sticking around once they've left school anyway, so what's the point?; and c) the locals beat up anyone with an English accent.

As soon as they leave school, they hot-foot it to the metropolis, probably one at least 400 miles away, making only rare visits back to the sticks (which they've always refused to call 'home') until they are middle-aged enough to burn out and flee the rat race and start the whole ball rolling all over again...

Q. Oh GOD, my 15-year-old daughter wants to have a party at our house. Since she brought it up I haven't slept, I've been so worried. I feel like I can't say no. What should I do?

A. You need draconian laws and the strength and courage to enforce them:

1 Issue numbered, laminated, if possible watermarked invitations making it clear that trespassers can expect to feel the full wrath of Dad and his air rifle.
2 Greet guests at the door yourself. Don't smile – it only encourages them. Insist they roll up their sleeves so you can check for track marks and empty their bags into the specially designated 'sharps' wheelie bin to your right.
3 Remain unobtrusive: there's a lot you can do nowadays with surveillance cameras and remote controls.
4 Ring-fence the designated party area, ideally with police incident tape. You really don't want alien teenagers using your expensive facial products.

'Middle age: When you begin to exchange your emotions for symptoms.'

Georges Clemenceau

OMG I FORGOT TO HAVE CHILDREN!

Though men can go on fathering children into their seventies (Charlie Chaplin fathered nine children after he was 50, his last when he was an impressive 73), women's fertility nose-dives after 35 (fewer eggs are produced and the uterus performs less effectively). Yet the number of women having children over 40 has nearly trebled from 9,336 in 1989 to 26,976 in 2009.

Having a baby could be your only chance these days of actually doing something fashionable.

But older parents are too tired to cope with a baby, and I'll practically be a pensioner before they're even at university.
Yes... there's something in that. But actually babies and children are tiring even if you're in your twenties. Anyone who's ever been on a car journey with one knows that.

As for being a pensioner – with the population becoming increasingly top-heavy (and we aren't talking about a boom in glamour modelling), you can forget any notions of retirement in the near future. Or pensions for that matter. Plus statistically, you'll be financially better off in your forties than in your twenties – and wiser. Which means you can spend your money on childcare while you have a nap.

What about the medical side?
Sadly, there are a few drawbacks: increased risks of premature birth, chromosomal abnormalities, miscarriage, ectopic pregnancy and stillbirth. And even if you're only in your early thirties, your hospital notes may refer to you as an 'old' or 'geriatric' primagravida, which doesn't do much for anyone's self-esteem.

Any role models?

Giving birth later is de rigueur for celebrity mums as it's a great way to get back in the papers. Madonna (41), Cherie Booth/Blair (45), Jane Seymour (45 – twins!), Holly Hunter (47 – twins again!), and, erm, the Countess of Wessex (42), to name but a few.

So how long have I got?

Technically, years. A 70-year-old Indian woman gave birth to twins in 2008; a Spanish woman had twin boys at 67 in 2006; a 67-year-old Romanian woman gave birth in 2005; an Italian woman gave birth aged 62 in 1995; Liz Buttle, from Wales, was 60 years old when she had her son in1997; and Elizabeth Adeney from Suffolk was 66 when she had her son Jolyon (meaning 'young at heart') in 2009. Sure, there's a chance you'll be dead before they finish university but at least you will get out of paying their fees.

- -

THE CONSOLATIONS OF REMAINING CHILD-FREE

Though your breeding friends* may try to convince you otherwise, it IS possible to remain child-free and still lead a happy and fulfilling life.

1 Children are a huge responsibility. Being a decent parent means facing up to this daily, even though there will be times when you want to – and in fact regularly do – stick them in front of the telly and go back to bed.

2 Children are expensive. According to recent research, it costs more than £200,000 to raise a child from birth to the age of 21. That takes in clothing, food, outings, holidays and (most draining of all) childcare. The cost peaks during the university years when you face paying out £14,000 a year.

3 You can go on long car journeys without having to listen to CDs of children's songs played on a 1987-vintage Casio keyboard by someone who failed their Grade 2 piano and sung by a woman whose chief ambition is seemingly to replace Carol Decker as lead singer of T'Pau, should Decker ever tire of hawking herself and her enormous hair round the 1980s revival circuit.

4 Children can be difficult. It starts with the Terrible Twos and continues until... actually, it just continues.

5 Children put a strain on your relationship. Haven't you wondered why so many of your friends are suddenly getting divorced within a few years of having kids?

* Obviously your breeding friends are painfully aware of the advantages of remaining child-free – there's nothing like having kids to remind you, on a daily basis, of the advantages of NOT having them. But if your friends are going to ruin their own lives, they are damn well going to ruin yours too.

**'The holy centaurs of the hills are vanished;
I have nothing but the embittered sun;
Banished heroic mother moon and vanished,
And now that I have come to fifty years
I must endure the timid sun.'**

WB Yeats, 'Lines Written in Dejection'

MIDLIFE ANTI-HERO:

Kenneth Widmerpool from
A Dance to the Music of Time

Widmerpool, one of the main characters in Anthony Powell's brilliant 12-book sequence, is a classic type: the cowardly and mediocre yet ambitious idiot whom no-one liked at school but who has, thanks to a combination of luck and opportunism, eclipsed you and all your contemporaries to become unthinkably powerful in his chosen sphere – often politics or the media. Every group has a Widmerpool somewhere on its periphery. He's the person you bitch about with your oldest friends after a long, long night out when you're too exhausted to hide the anger and disappointment that's eating you up. Because your Widmerpool never goes away. Indeed, the degrees of separation between you and him may decrease alarmingly: your paths may even cross at a wedding or reunion. When they do, he will patronise you to death. And you will always hate him.

4.
HOUSE & GARDEN

As you no longer have the time, energy or childcare to go out, nor your finger sufficiently on the cultural pulse to know where to go or what to see if you did, your home has become the focus of your world – restaurant, cinema, office, classroom, gym, study, library, art gallery, junk storage unit… Which is why it's perfectly natural to obsess over things like scented candles and fish kettles in lieu of having an actual life.

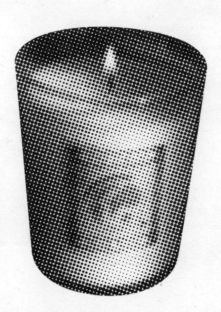

THE MIDLIFE DREAM HOME

When you got your first place, you had nothing to furnish it with save a camping stove, a futon and some Reject Shop crockery in primary colours.

Now, however, you've got far too much stuff, and have long ago replaced the crockery, futon and camping stove. But these days you want *quality*. You want craftsmanship. You want character. You want a handmade oak table that's been sanded to perfection and a pepper mill with a state-of-the-art grinder.

Marketing people reel you in with phrases like 'dream kitchen', but have you ever stopped to ask yourself: 'When was the last time I had a dream about a kitchen?'

To help you construct the ultimate midlife home, we've put together a checklist:

Kitchen:

Le Creuset casserole dish (denoting that you now cook grown-up things needing more than two ingredients)

Serious pepper grinder (preferably with grinding mechanism engineered by someone who also designs cars)

Teapot (even if you use tea bags when you're on your own, guests require a teapot and choice of teas)

Aga (those who live or aspire to live in the country); Smeg (those who think they're chic and urban)

A breadmaker/slow cooker (which you've dug out from the back of the cupboard now that you have to economise to pay the school fees)

A fish kettle (still working out what to do with it)

A double sink (preferably Belfast. How can anyone live with just a single sink? Where can you pour the teapot dregs?)

Under-floor heating (which will have just about heated the concrete six hours after you turn it on)

Task lighting under cabinets (because your eyesight is already going)

An apron (delivered with your veg box)

A knife block (probably a wedding present – because why else would you spend good money for a block of wood?) And a proper sharpener, of course

Area of wall painted with blackboard paint (to draw up everyone's weekly schedule and write messages to members of your household you never see)

Living room:

A chair whose designer you can name (eg an Eames lounger or Matthew Hilton Balzac chair and footstool)

Jo Malone/Diptyque scented candles (please tell us you haven't used joss sticks for years)

Very expensive speakers (Bose, Kharma, Wisdom, Marten… nothing less than a grand)

Proper art (alongside your own black-and-white photos of Whitstable beach blown up and framed)

A standard lamp (turning on the main overhead light, rather than creating light 'pools' with lamps, dimmer switches and uplighters, is harsh and unflattering to both you and the room)

Bespoke shelving (by that great Oxbridge-educated carpenter you met at a dinner party)

Bedroom:

A proper sprung bed (as the nice man in John Lewis pointed out, we spend more of our lives in bed than anywhere else, so this really should be your most important domestic purchase)

Wallpaper (if you live in a city, keep it to one wall only, as featured in interiors mags)

A quilt/bedspread (somehow the bed has started to seem naked without one)

Proper wooden coat-hangers (at some point by now you'll have read an article stressing the importance of looking after your clothes properly)

An extra sofa/armchair (ostensibly for lying on and reading Elizabeth Barrett Browning-style, more probably piled with washing you haven't had time to out away)

Bathroom:

Heated towel rail (anything drying on radiators screams student flatshare)

Mood lighting (installed back when you thought you'd have time to linger in the bath surrounded by scented candles and classical music)

A spare radio (permanently tuned to R4 so that you can catch the *Today* programme while you do your teeth)

A free-standing bath (salvaged and redipped, or sculptural stone selected from the classifieds in *Elle Deco*)

Home office:

Piles of unfiled bills (next to empty hanging files)

Dumped sports equipment (squash racquet, mini dumb bells and other signs of good intentions)

DIY shelving (when you were trying to save money and thought it couldn't be *that* difficult)

Cheap sofabed (relegated from living room when you bought the Heal's one, now used when a parent comes to stay, under the pretence of helping with the children, although they spend the whole time complaining about how uncomfortable it is)

Computer (bought for yourself for homeworking/business plan/writing novel, used by everyone else for online shopping, homework help and computer games)

A small portable telly (with aerial and video slot, highlighting the fact that a) you are in denial about digital takeover, and b) you have already seen both the innovation and the death of video tape in your lifetime)

Magnetic notice board (because you're scared those common stickytacks will ruin the walls)

A ridiculously elaborate, and now unused, burglar alarm programmed with the date of your anniversary

Things you should have ditched by now
clip frames
novelty anything
wine bottles used as candlesticks
lava lamp
exposed clothes rail
anything pine
Che Guevara/music poster (unless original print)
woodwork painted in rainbow colours

HANDY HOUSEHOLD HINTS YOUR MOTHER WOULD HAVE TOLD YOU IF SHE HADN'T BEEN TOO BUSY FIGHTING THE SEXUAL REVOLUTION

To clean a burnt aluminium saucepan, boil water in it with an onion added.

Use old newspapers as cloths to get a good shine on windows.

Use glycerine to remove coffee stains.

Keep moths away with cloves.

Keep flies out of the kitchen with a windowbox of mint. They hate it.

Use baby oil on a soft cloth to remove smears from stainless steel, chrome or aluminium.

To remove the smell of cigarettes from a room, leave a bowl of water out overnight – this will absorb the unpleasant odours.

When using lemon for a drink or in cooking, put the discarded outer part in the sink to keep it smelling fresh.

To remove stains from the carpet, rub first with a slice of potato

-----

DIY TIPS YOUR FATHER TRIED TO PASS ON WHEN YOU WERE TOO BUSY FASHIONING YOURSELF AS A NEW MAN

If the chimney catches fire, put damp newspaper over the coals – the resulting steam will extinguish the flames.

When wiring a plug remember: brown is live, blue is neutral, and the stripy yellow and green one is earth. Live goes to the right, into the bit with the fuse, neutral goes round to the left and earth goes in the middle.

Before painting new wood, paint over the knots with knotting solution to prevent the sap bleeding through subsequent coats of paint.

Use a mixture of five parts water to one part PVA glue to seal a flaky wall before plastering or painting over. This aids bonding of the new plaster.

If you are opening up an old fireplace, make sure there is a lintel (horizontal piece of stone) above the opening to support the mantel piece and bricks above it.

When sealing round the edges of the bath, half fill the bath with water before piping out the sealant. If you don't, the first time you run a bath, the weight of the water will pull the sealant away from the wall.

To change the washer on a dripping tap, turn off water at the mains, unscrew and remove the 'headgear' (bit above the tap arm), reach in and swap the old O-ring (circular washer) with a new one. Or pay a plumber £45.

Further reading: *DIY Know How with Show How* by Julian Cassell and Peter Parham

---

JOHN LEWIS

Ah, *John Lewis!* Even the name is like sipping chamomile tea while you relax in your favourite armchair, warming your toes in front of an open fire. Nothing can possibly go wrong when you're in John Lewis. There's just something so reassuring about a place where they call you 'Sir' or 'Madam', where the staff actually know about the things they're selling (watch them get quite animated about pocket-sprung mattress technology, for example), where the toilets are clean and plentiful, and where they know the proper names for everyday items like *escutcheons* (those metal surrounds and flaps that cover your keyhole), *jiggers* (those cup things for measuring gin for cocktails) and *ric-rac* (that wiggly stuff that people sew along the bottom of things for decoration).

Many people in their twenties foolishly shun John Lewis, considering it to be old and fusty compared to its glamorous London neighbours such as Selfridges. But then they find themselves in need of proper sherry glasses, napkin rings or a crochet hook, and don't know where to turn. 'John Lewis, of course!' say their wise elders. And so they discover this haven of 200-thread Egyptian cotton bed linen, bone china soup plates, pelmets, trouser presses, slow cookers, lint rollers, pin cushions and more than 30 different types of pepper mill.

Even when you're buying the uniform for you daughter's independent school you can appease your left-wing demons with the knowledge that John Lewis is a model of socialism – all permanent employees are, famously, partners in the business. See, everything works out in John Lewis.

- -

IKEA

Alternatively, there's Ikea.

While the queues of bickering families with trolleys piled with quirky chairs and rubber plants have been likened to one of the Circles of Hell (perhaps one specially set aside for Wrath and Tightfistedness), on the plus side, you get to dine on meatballs in gravy; feel like a proper artisan as you screw the furniture together yourself; ask for products called Umpalømpåh, Lusty and Scräg; and impulse-buy bumper packs of napkins, cheap glassware, CD racks, and scatter cushions even though you actually only went to look at kitchens.

Devotees will tell you with pride that the Billy bookcase is a bona fide design classic, with more than 41 million sold and counting. And it's incredible to think that, prior to 1987, the UK was blissfully unaware of lingonberries, Allen keys or pits of coloured plastic balls. And because Ikea is named after its founder Ingvar Kamprad, the farm he grew up on – Elmtaryd – and the village he is from – Agunnaryd – it makes it feel, you know, really personal, as if by shopping there you are part of one big family.

Some people try to avoid it. Some over-indulge and for a while go cold turkey. Some people think they are above it. But then these people find themselves in need of a really cheap sofabed or giant bag of Dime bars, and once more that distinctive blue-and-yellow sign beckons…

CONVERSIONS AND EXTENSIONS

There's nothing like a bit of gratuitous building work to reinvigorate your relationship with your home and eat up any surplus cash. The most common projects for the restless homeowner are: loft, conservatory, basement, side return/kitchen extension, porch, garage conversion.

Whichever you go for, expect confrontation with neighbours who have so much time on their hands that they can acquaint themselves with the finer points of the Town and Country Planning (General Permitted Development) Order 1995 with the simple aim of putting you to the expense and inconvenience of reducing your domed roof light by five inches because they've taken exception to the fact that you've had a loft extension because you couldn't afford to move to a bigger house, *even though it's exactly the same domed roof light that's on every loft extension in the vicinity*, leading to years of petty feuding until one sunny Sunday afternoon one of you stabs the other with a pair of secateurs over a dispute about the height of a hedge...

THERE'S NO SUCH THING AS WHITE

By now you ought to be sophisticated enough to realise *there is no such thing as white*.

There is All White, Strong White, Wimborne White, Great White and James White (Farrow & Ball). There is Marble White, Birch White and Boulder White (Sanderson). There is Shirting, Slaked Lime and Echo (Little Greene). Or Old Towel and Spilt Milk.

So do not imagine you can get away with just painting your home 'white'. You can choose an industrial paint for covering large areas such as ceilings (there's no point wasting money), and something functional like Dulux Kitchens and Bathrooms or an eggshell for rooms that need to be wipe-clean and mould-free. But for goodness' sake pay attention to pigmentation when it comes to hallways and living rooms.

The pigment might be ever so slightly bluish, greyish, reddish or creamy. Your less aesthetically inclined friends will cry 'Emperor's new clothes!' and swear they can't tell the difference between one test pot and another.

They don't realise it's all about *quality of light*. Indeed, it's scientifically proven that flat white is tiring on the eye. And doesn't your watercolour of north Norfolk look so much more vibrant hung against a tone?

Meanwhile, if you're looking for a dark colour for the front door, might we steer you away from black towards Off-Black, Pitch Black, Black Blue, Downpipe, Dark Beaver, Railings…

LEARN TO LOVE HOUSEWORK

One minute you're an ambitious young thing, out all the time and communicating with your flatmate via fridge notes about whose turn it is to do the washing-up; the next you're old and domesticated, cutting out drawer liners and admiring the whiteness of your wash.

It's unclear exactly when you started to treat housework like an art, but doubtless your interest increased as your social life and career prospects diminished.

Housework constitutes a bonding experience with your home, and the realisation that you are too old to live in a student slum. New concerns that your younger self would have ridiculed as a waste of time include:

• ironing items that cannot actually be seen by anyone other than you – sheets, handkerchiefs, vests;
• buying extreme cleaning products such as caustic soda, carpet freshener, laundry-whiteners and dishwasher deodoriser;
• knowing which vacuum cleaner attachment does what;
• confidently using more than one setting on your washing machine;
• rationalising the family hat, scarf and gloves box;
• washing the cloth shopping bags rather than just waiting for them to fall apart.

It is important, however, that you know when you've gone too far. Descaling the kettle occasionally is admirable; admiring yourself in a new pinny means it's time to seek help.

ARE FISH-BONING TWEEZERS STRICTLY NECESSARY?

By midlife, you'll have acquired a mass of gratuitous kitchen gadgets – relics from those distant pre-kids days when you had the money to buy things impulsively, things you didn't strictly need. Like avocado pitters, professional potato ricers, grape scissors or fish-boning tweezers.

The reasons the kitchen throws up so many opportunities for pointless spending are easily summarised:

• Men like gadgets. Having gadgets in the kitchen encourages them to cook.
• Having the right knives is a sign that you take food seriously, and taking food seriously is a sign that you've moved on from your bedsit days and are now a proper grown-up.
• It allows trends analysts to come up with terms like 'kitchenalia'.
• It allows couples who've been together years to find something to get their partner for their birthday.

Specialist cutlery you may secretly lust after includes: grapefruit knives with a kink at the end; sweetcorn skewers; oyster shuckers; caviar spoons; one of those long pokey things for pulling whelks from their shells... You may end up serving a rather peculiar menu to get them all in, but it will be extremely satisfying.

THE MODERN WORLD EXPLAINED:
HOW TO TURN ON A TELEVISION

Find remote control. No, not that one – that's for the DVD player. You want the flimsy grey one with the squidgy buttons.

Point remote control at TV. Now press the red button in the top right-hand corner, the one with the funny circle-broken-by-vertical-line ident on it. You may have to keep your finger on it for several seconds while your TV works out what you're trying to do.

TROUBLESHOOTING: Have you switched the TV on at the mains? Have you put your contact lenses in?

Turn on the Freeview box you bought four years ago after that nice man in Currys assured you it was the future of television.

Your box wants to be friends with your TV! Help it along by finding the AV button on your remote control. A drop-down 'source' menu should appear on the screen. Using the arrows, move the pointer down to EXT1. Then press the right arrow key to select it.

Try it again.

Okay, turn everything off then on again and repeat steps 1 to 4.

You can't tell what channel it is because only half the channel info bar is visible at the bottom of the screen? Hmm – sounds like there's a conflict between the box and the TV and it's affecting the default settings for aspect ratio.

Don't be rude, I *am* speaking English. Find the button on your remote with the ident that looks like a screen being stretched.

Look harder, it's there somewhere. Maybe it isn't a screen, maybe it's... oh, I don't know. Your TV's a Philips, isn't it? I could tell you if it was a Sony. Buy a new TV! Yours is an antique anyway. It isn't even proper HD.

MIDLIFE MILESTONE: **KEEPING A GUEST ROOM**

Being able to offer space in 'the spare room' is a sign that, domestically, you are a grown-up. A spare room is an open invitation to old friends who've moved to another town, should they ever make good on their promise to come and visit. But it also stands for the option of live-in childcare; the threat of banishment in the heat of a marital tiff; and the possibility that, should you and your friends ever again be able to schedule a mutually convenient date for a night of hell-raising, you'll be able to offer them somewhere comfortable to bed down.

You may also feel the compulsion to invest in special guest towels, duplicate bedding and a low-grade guest radio. But do draw the line at spare toothbrushes and tiny guest soaps you've nicked from hotels and aeroplane toilets.

Unfortunately, a spare room is rarely spare for long, and often finds itself commandeered for other midlife aspirations: reading room, music room, laundry room, dressing room, art room, home cinema, playroom, dungeon or sauna. Or, more commonly, is just filled with junk.

For those unable to maintain a fully furnished guest room all year round, there is now a whole industry based around temporary bedding solutions beyond the first-flat futon or Z-bed (trust us, you really don't want to sleep on a Z-bed at your age, and futons are a bit 1996): the truckle bed which is rolled out on casters and pops up to become a single bed that's probably comfier than your own; top-of-the-range, no-pumping-necessary, self-inflating mattresses such as the Aerobed (ideal for comfortable camping); or pull-down wall beds for a 007 frisson that makes you feel like you're still a carefree bachelor.

SUBURBIA

In your disaffected youth, the suburbs signified everything you wanted to rebel against, particularly if you lived in them. Conformity and uniformity reigned over the houses, the streets, the people; the jobs they did and the views they held. At the time, you were with Paul Weller (or XTC, or Blur) and Julian Barnes (or Hanif Kureishi, or Richard Ford) – raging against the tedium of it all, desperate to escape from the land of *Terry and June* and *Abigail's Party*.

Only now do you appreciate the masterpieces of town planning that are Letchworth and Welwyn Garden City. Besides, it's quite nice to have a garden. And a shed. And a drive. And a bit of peace and quiet. And you've been able to buy a whole house for what you got for your Fulham flat.

People can mock all they like, but you're not going to be like your parents, trimming the privet and washing the car at the weekends, sipping sweet sherry with the neighbours. You're going to live!

Mind you, aren't you just so *tired* at the weekends? You're commuting all week, so you really don't want to go into town on your day off. You just want to put your feet up. Or go for a gentle walk. And the car is looking a bit grubby. All the green space is such a relief. It's almost like being in the country. Almost.

The schools are good, so that's a weight off your mind. With a little help from a private tutor, the kids are bound to get into St Swithin's.

And don't think the city is the only place you can get culture. There's a characterful little gallery run by two nice women. One does pots, the other watercolours. They serve teas, too. And the Mundania Players put on what everyone agreed was a really good version of Tom Stoppard's *The Real Thing* last month. One of the cast actually used to be an actor...

WHERE TO LIVE...

...to exploit the grammar school system
As children approach school age, Londoners in particular head for the suburban ring and Home Counties. Of the top performing state schools, a disproportionate number are in Kent (Tonbridge, Sevenoaks, Bexleyheath, Orpington, Dartford) and Essex (Colchester, Chelmsford, Saffron Walden).

...to bring up kids
Chorlton, Manchester. Relaxed, creative types come here to spawn. Both the grocers and the toy shop are run as cooperatives, and the newsagent on Beech Road sells more copies of the *Guardian* than anywhere else in the UK. Primary schools are so competitive, it's often siblings only, and even then they might only be accommodated through the addition of a bulge class.

...for an easy commute
Cambridge allows you to still work in London if you need to but feel smug about cycling everywhere without having to encounter hills or the Elephant & Castle roundabout at rush hour. Plus it has its own John Lewis.

...for genteel city life
Have the bright lights of Glasgow started to scorch your retina? Step down a gear in Edinburgh. Voted best place to live in UK 2007 by C4's *Location, Location, Location*

...to buy your weekend house so that the locals can't afford to
Anywhere

...for networking
The golf courses of Hertfordshire (Hadley Wood, Rickmansworth, Borehamwood) and Surrey (Esher, St George's Hill) see as much business done as the boardrooms of the City

...to embrace early retirement
The Isles of Scilly have the highest proportion of over-50s – 52.4%. (Greenwich, London, has the lowest at 25.5%).

...to fulfil your dream of opening your own bookshop
Hay-on-Wye famously has one bookshop for every 36 residents (and the clock from the title sequence of *Antiques Roadshow*). It can probably squeeze in another.

...to live like a rock star
Manchester may be the beating heart of the nation's music scene, but all the bands live in Macclesfield, its affluent neighbour to the south. Doves, New Order, one of the Stone Roses, and, er, Noddy Holder. Ian Curtis (Joy Division) died there in 1980. It's in the top ten places paying most tax in Britain.

...to retire with your civil partner
Hebden Bridge in the Yorkshire Dales is the self-proclaimed lesbian capital of Britain, chocca with Victorian terraces and vegan cafés. There's even a lesbian bird-watching society and hill-walking group.

...to get away from it all, but still run your highly successful clothing catalogue/veg box scheme/organic yoghurt company/seafood restaurant
Devon.

...to really get away from it all
Foula in the Shetlands is the most remote British island to be inhabited all year round. It has 30 residents, but you will have to learn to knit. Or fish.

5.
SEX & RELATIONSHIPS

In your twenties, relationships are clear, gently rippling streams filled with playful trout and capering beetles. But then midlife strikes and they are TRANSFORMED into polluted creeks whose fetid black water is carpeted in thick algae not unlike the slime that destroys the Liberator in the final episode of *Blake's 7*. What, as Lenin once asked, is to be done?

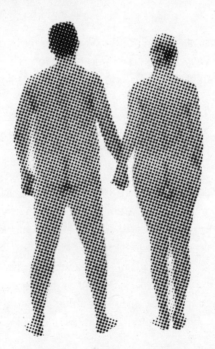

ROMANTIC EVENINGS IN...

First, get yourself a DVD box set of a programme everyone was talking about six months (or even six years) ago but which you never found the time/energy to watch when it was on. Lengthy US drama series (*The West Wing, The Wire, Mad Men*) are a popular choice, being too complicated for your now-failing short-term memory to recall from week to week and so easier to follow in batches of three.

Alternatively, opt for a nostalgia fest of good British comedy (*Dad's Army, Yes, Minister*) or drama that appears to have been made for adults and doesn't do that swoopy, speeded-up, ITV Drama Premiere flash-cutting thing every ten seconds (*House of Cards, Edge of Darkness, Boys From the Blackstuff*). These will have been given to you as a Christmas present by your other half or in-laws because no one knows what to get you these days or can be arsed to think about it.

Avoid foreign films with subtitles. Although when you met you both pretended to be into independent/world cinema to impress each other, frankly, if you wanted to spend the evening reading you'd go to bed with a book.

The beauty of the box set is that it will also give you something in common now that you both have different friends, different hobbies and different workplaces.

After you've finished supper and loaded the dishwasher, adjourn to the sofa with a bottle of wine and a bar of Green & Black's. Place your mobiles on either arm of the sofa to ensure that you can both respond to emails, laugh at Facebook posts by people your partner doesn't know and bid for vintage valve radios on eBay throughout the programme viewing. On no account should one person 'get ahead' on episodes or the entire fragile equilibrium of the relationship will be thrown into jeopardy, taking years to realign.

'BECAUSE ULTIMATELY WE'RE JUST ANIMALS...'

What you mean is: 'Animals don't stay together, do they? Animals aren't monogamous.' That's your justification for random shagging around. But what if *all your assumptions about the animal world were wrong*? What would you do then, eh? Eh? Consider:

Coyotes: both parents feed the weaned pups with regurgitated food. Sometimes coyotes mate with wolves and domestic dogs.

Bears: the male bear leaves the female shortly after mating. He will kill and sometimes eat any bear cub he comes across, even if he's the father.

Flatworm fish: they're monogamous. But they don't have much choice in the matter: their bodies actually fuse during sex. Imagine!

Beavers: they're *reasonably* monogamous, and will generally stay together until a partner dies, which could be a while: beavers can live for up to 24 years. The daddy beaver shows the baby beaver how to build a dam. Sweet!

Gibbons: only 6% of primates are monogamous. Gibbons live in small families with up to four offspring. The mummy gibbon is in charge. Gibbon couples like to sing together – though not 'Funky Gibbon' by The Goodies.

Bonobos: will shag anything – young or old, male or female. Apparently, it's a 'means of greeting and resolving conflicts'. Well, they would say that, wouldn't they?

Dolphins: now this will surprise you. God knows, it surprised us. Dolphins mate several times a day. That's why they're so happy! Also, dolphin sex is brisk and functional and, frequently, gay. Sometimes, dolphins behave sexually towards humans. (Insert 'Free Willy' joke here. Or was Willy a whale?)

KEEPING THE MAGIC ALIVE

Is your relationship getting as stale as that Fortnum & Mason 'Gamekeeper's Fruit Cake' someone gave you after your hernia op but which the kids spat out because it 'tasted like soil'? Why not try:

• Helping your (male) partner transfer all his old vinyl and cassettes onto iTunes using that crappy USB device he saw advertised in the back of the *Telegraph* magazine.
• Helping your (female) partner take all her 'winter' clothes to the dry cleaners and take out her 'summer' wardrobe from the drawers under the divan in the attic.
• Christ, what next... Dressing up in each other's clothes. What about that?
• Do something neither of you has ever done before, together. Drystone walling? Cleaning out the car?
• Or one of you could learn to *fly*! Yes YES! Then you could, on a whim, jet off to Le Touquet for romantic weekends!
• Did you know the resort of Le Touquet was created in 1876 by the founder of top French newspaper *Le Figaro*? Before he got hold of it, it was just sand dunes and forest.
• Sand sand sand... Ah, got it! You could get a big sandpit and play in it like people do on management training courses in bad comic novels.
• Do gamekeepers even eat fruit cake?
• Imagine if Richard Desmond founded a resort. What would that look like?
• There's always porn.

- -

MARRIAGE À LA MIDLIFE

It you didn't get married when you were young, it was probably because:
a) you hadn't met the right person; b) you were ideologically opposed to such an outmoded patriarchal system; c) you were too busy backpacking; d) you couldn't afford it; e) it was still illegal for same-sex couples; or f) you *were* married, but to someone else.

Some people like to keep it this way. We've got this far, they think, what's the point? We've already got kids, and a full set of cutlery. Such people (eg Emma Freud) continue to call their partner of 20 years (ie Richard Curtis) their 'boyfriend' because they know it sounds odd and annoys people.

The most romantic reason to get married is because you don't have to. More practically, however, it gives the father paternity rights over his own children and, as long as you do it in your forties, the bride can get in under the wire of still looking vaguely fresh-faced in the photos. It's also a great excuse to get all your friends together for a party that doesn't involve helium-filled balloons emblazoned with your age.

• Keep the ceremony low-key. Local register office says 'we haven't completely sold out'. And if you already have two kids, the vicar of the pretty parish church might question your religious convictions.

• Dress: no one over 40 is going to get away with a full-on meringue. Or a train. Keep your outfit well cut and expensive. And remember to wear big pants to hold it all in. A modest veil, however, is acceptable, not so much to hide your virginal modesty as your frown lines. (Same-sex couples can get away with more in the way of flamboyance).

• Bridesmaids: your own children will want first refusal. This is okay, as long as they're not teenagers as this will make you look old.

• Who to give you away? Tricky one. By this stage you may no longer have the full complement of parents. Alternatively, if your mum and dad did that partner swap with the couple from the village, you may have a surplus. Play the 'independent woman' card and refuse to be given away.

• Stag do : cricket, tequila and falling out over issues of political ideology.

• Hen night: spa, prosecco and falling out because the maid of honour once snogged the groom in 1992 and the bride didn't know.

• Honeymoon: either a child-friendly destination (visiting Santa in Lapland, Disneyland Paris) or a night in a fancy hotel while the mother-in-law babysits.

TOP FIVE WORST MIDLIFE DATE MOVIES

1 *Heartburn (1986)*
Based on Nora Ephron's book about her marriage to Watergate hero Carl Bernstein. Most notable for the scene in which Meryl Streep whacks her philandering husband Jack Nicholson in the face with a key-lime pie at a friend's dinner party, then says: 'Can I have the car keys, please?' Messy!

2 *Scenes from a Marriage* (1973)
Edited-down version of six-part series made for Swedish TV by laureate of pain Ingmar Bergman. Lovely Liv Ullmann plays a woman thrown into despair and confusion by the discovery that her husband is having an affair. Wince-making!

3 *Husbands and Wives* (1992)
Last good film by Woody Allen. When couple Sally and Jack announce their break-up, their friends Gabe and Judy (Allen and his ex-wife Mia Farrow, respectively) start examining their own marriage more closely: 'You'd never say you were putting your diaphragm on... and then not do it, right?' Excruciating!

4 *Kramer vs Kramer* (1979)
Meryl Streep (again! She's so good at divorcees...) leaves Dustin Hoffman to bring up their son, returns 15 months later to contest custody – and SPOILER ALERT!!!!!!!!!! succeeds, thanks to the 'tender years doctrine' then prevalent in US divorce trials which said young children were better off with their mothers. Heart-rending!

5 *The Squid and the Whale* (2005)
Low-budget account of director Noah Baumbach's memories of his childhood in 1980s Brooklyn, specifically the spitefully competitive non-relationship between his freshly divorced parents. Hilarious!

MIDLIFE SEX TIPS

1 Make sure both of you are in the same room and that the lights are dimmed.
2 Remove your clothes. All of them.
3 Or yes, you can remove each other's, but that's really going to drag things out and besides, all you'll get for your efforts is a volley of protest along the lines of 'Your hands are freezing!' and 'You're tickling me' and 'Not like that – look, it sort of unhooks'.
4 Stay awake! It's 11.45, admittedly – you spent half the evening supervising homework and the other half sorting washing – but once you start worrying about time, it's all over.
5 Relax.
6 You see? It's okay once you get into it.
7 *What's that noise*? It's not one of the kids out of bed, is it? Relax, relax: what if it is? They're probably just going to the toilet. They'll go straight back to bed.
8 Whatever you do, DON'T SAY ANYTHING. And don't go 'Sshhh'.
9 You've been asked if anything's the matter! Amber alert! Say no, nothing, it's all great, mmm, etc.
10 Oh Christ, the door's opening...

THE MIDLIFE AFFAIR

Grip your fedora with both hands. A recentish survey by incomprehensible young persons' television channel BBC3 found that one in seven people had been unfaithful to their current partner. Now, BBC3's target audience is 16 to 34, so its opinions on most matters can be cheerfully disregarded. But this figure sounds about right – if anything, it's a little on the low side. (Consider your own friends and how many of them you know to be playing around.)

Midlifers have affairs because they're bored and think their lives ought to be more exciting than they are. Adultery, in this context, acquires a thrilling glamour. Even the word itself is glamorous, with its connotations of husky-voiced dames knocking back bourbon in smoky bars and built-in acknowledgement that what's going on is adult and consensual: not for BBC Three viewers, whose infidelities are unlikely to extend much further than snogging Jason from Year 9 on the geography field trip.

Midlife affairs fall into six distinct categories:

1 One-off restorative diversions (after which normal service is resumed).
2 Guilty fumbles (usually drunken and involving a work colleague or someone from a school committee because, let's face it, who else do you ever meet these days?)
3 Cries for help (which usually end in stalking).
4 Repeat offences of the long-distance philanderer.
5 Mundane suburbiana (wife-swapping, 'open marriages', dogging etc).
6 The final severance (usually associated with midlife crisis).

What should you do if you discover your partner has had or is having an affair? First, flick them with a wet towel. Then, try to work out which type of affair it is. If it's 6, chances are you'll have been told about it and are already consulting lawyers. If it's 5, you may well be involved too, in which case all we can say is EURRRGHHH!! But cunning practitioners of 4 may attempt to convince you that their offence is a lesser-grade 1, 2 or 3 – excusable, up to a point, and nothing a couple of sessions of counselling won't sort.

The problem with 4 is not just that serial philanderers are sociopathic freaks who shouldn't be given house room – it's that 4 often leads to 5 in the most hilarious (or not, depending on where you're sitting) development of all: the May–December romance in which both parties, but particularly the older one, run around telling everyone (or at least those few people who are still talking to them) that THIS IS IT, it's NEVER HAPPENED TO THEM BEFORE, not like this: they are IN LOVE, going to have (more) children, etc!! Oh yes.

Practitioners of 1, 2 and 3 are often forgiven because, when pressed, they come up with perfectly good reasons for their Hugh Grant-style 'moment of madness' – sorrow at loss of intimacy, depression at advancing age, feeling unattractive and underappreciated. Serial philanderers, however, are typically unreflective alpha males for whom 'Regret' is merely a song by New Order which they liked because the band performed it for *Top of the Pops* on the set of *Baywatch*.

How to tell if your partner is having an affair:

1 They have a glassy, faraway look in their eyes, as if they have been 'chosen' by a sinister cult.
2 They spend hours sniggering over their BlackBerry and when you ask 'What?' shake their heads in an I-couldn't-possibly-explain-this-type-of-humour-to-you sort of way. Then they lock themselves in the bathroom. With their BlackBerry. For 20 minutes. Whispering to themselves. For 20 minutes. Jesus.
3 They start going to the gym when the only previous interest they've shown in exercise was the for-charity 'cake-a-thon' at your kids' school where you won a meal for two at Café Rouge if you ate 15 Mr Kipling Fondant Fancies in three minutes.
4 They start ordering DVD box sets of critically acclaimed US TV dramas which

you suggested watching months ago. Your partner, back then: 'Oh God, do we have to? It's so blah blah, cops in Baltimore, drugs, "realistic scenes of urban life", depressing blah blah.' You question this U-turn and are rewarded with feeble, reedy-voiced flannelling along the lines of, 'Someone told me it was really good.' 'I DID!' you say. 'I TOLD YOU IT WAS GOOD!' And they look at you as if they've never seen you before and ask, 'Did you?'

5 They stink of sex even though you haven't had it for ages.

Affairs: pros and cons

Pros:
- Sex with someone new is fun.
- They make you feel younger.
- They make you feel like you've got a pulse.
- They make office life more interesting, assuming your shagee is a work colleague.
- They make office life more interesting for your colleagues: what, you thought you'd managed to keep it secret?
- You might get promoted.
- Sex with someone new is fun. Oh hang on, we've had that one...
- You might get bought dinner into the bargain. No one's bought you dinner for ages.
- If it 'goes permanent', you might end up in a better relationship than the one you're currently in. God, that sounds callous, doesn't it?

Cons:
- Sex with someone new is fun for a bit, then it's like normal sex – which you got bored with, remember?
- Another human being might have to see you naked – someone who hasn't seen you naked before.
- Affairs almost always end badly.
- Like, in divorce and stuff.

- Just because you *feel* younger doesn't mean you *are* younger.
- You could be doing something more constructive instead – like helping your children with their homework, you selfish, narcissistic cretin.
- It's a midlife crisis cliché. And you hate clichés.
- You've forgotten what to do.

INTERNET DATING

Why not spend an evening you'll never get back with a duplicitous sociopath? Actually, hang on...

The standard line on internet dating is that it's no big deal, that everyone does it – even that it's 'a bit of fun'. The truth is, though, that if your skin is any thinner than saddle leather or you have a tendency towards existential melancholy – if, as Timothy Spall once said of himself, you occasionally shed a tear in Sainsbury's – it should not be entered into lightly, if at all.

There is one thing to be said for it. Even taking into account the numbers of liars and blaggards in its ranks, it does give access to far more single 32–38-year-olds who live within five miles, want children and like Elbow, than you could find in the real world. For those wearily familiar with the experience of going to a party and summoning up the nerve to talk to the only attractive and apparently unattached person there, only for said person's partner to appear and slip his hand into hers, it can feel like wilful self-sabotage not to sign up.

But this strength is also its weakness. Being constantly reminded of the thousands of possible mates out there encourages lack of commitment, similar to when you're on a picnic and can't settle in one spot because it might be even lovelier around the corner. Furthermore, interactions begun online are subject to unwritten laws whereby you can be dropped at any stage of the proceedings, after one email or four dates, without apology or explanation. As it is with abuse, this behaviour is repeated by the victim, and brutality prevails. Men will find that all the pretty girls are oversubscribed and won't even bother reading their message. Women will discover that most of the men want women younger than they are.

You must be careful not to appear to care about any of this, though, because if you do you're 'a nutter'.

- -

MIDLIFE CONUNDRUM: **WHEN DOES SPINSTERHOOD START?**

Obviously, it's every girl's dream to meet the right man, settle down, have lots of kids, run the house, juggle that with a career, quietly scream inside and go slowly insane... You say this to your mother, wondering if you've got your irony level set high enough. For good measure, you complain a bit about smug marrieds and outmoded cultural conventions. But it's no good. She still doesn't believe you when you tell her you're perfectly happy on your own and you don't need a man, and you're not a lesbian, and your sister can supply her with grandchildren, so why can't she just be proud of all your other achievements?

Just because you're wedded to the single life, it doesn't mean you have to fall into the traditional categories: cat-loving spinster or Bridget Jones. But to ensure people see you as the complex, three-dimensional creature you are, you might want to throw a few stones in the path of their stereotyping.

Do you, for instance, have more than two of the following?

- Organic shoes
- A hedgehog you feed
- Three stray cats you've informally adopted
- Dirty washing on your bathroom floor
- Your own kiln
- A gay male best friend
- Tweed hiking trousers
- A wine box in the fridge

TILL LIFE US DO PART...

One in three marriages ends in divorce. But that's not how it seems in midlife. In midlife, EVERY marriage seems to end in divorce, and every long-term, might-as-well-be-married-but-we-don't-approve-of-it relationship in aggrieved separation.

From the point of view of the passive onlooker, it's a domino effect that begins in your late thirties. Within five years, your functioning, broadly happy relationship looks weird and anomalous. And you may well ask yourself: What makes me so different? Am I blind to (or absurdly tolerant of) my partner's faults? Or am I a coward, content to sit out a sub-standard marriage because ending it is too stressful and expensive to contemplate? Is my sex drive as strong as it should be? If it were stronger, which is to say properly strong, wouldn't I be more interested than I am in, well, chasing novelty? What am I repressing?

Other people's separations can be disorientating. Couples you regarded as friends with happy lives must secretly have hated each other! Everything you thought you knew was wrong. That time David and Sue came for dinner and you had a nice evening reminiscing about Glastonbury in the mid '90s (you saw Robbie Williams clowning around with Oasis), and Sue brought a rubbish rhubarb crumble and David gave you tax advice, and at the end everyone was laughing and saying, 'We must do this again soon' – it was all a SHAM. Afterwards, when they got in the car, David and Sue DIDN'T TALK. They drove home in SILENCE, and when they got there they SLUNK OFF TO SEPARATE BEDROOMS, pausing only to SCOWL at each other and say simultaneously, 'I'm having the first shower tomorrow morning.'

The flipside of this is those car-crash couples whose demise you've been predicting for years. They're more satisfying to observe. Actually, it's a stronger sensation than satisfaction: it's a ROSY GLOW OF CLASS-A SCHADENFREUDE.

What, though, if you're planning on getting divorced yourself? Here are some tried-and-tested tips to remember:

1 When communicating the decision, make sure you send clear signals to your partner, who may be in shock or denial. For example: 'I am leaving you because you bore me senseless' or 'I haven't fancied you since before the children were born'.

2 When telling the children, who will feel bewildered and frightened by your decision, it's kinder not to say: 'For God's sake, you're 19! We brought you up together, didn't we? What's all the fuss? What do you think this is, *The Waltons*?'

3 Take time before introducing a new partner to your children. And when you do, don't say, 'You can call him Daddy if you like. I'm sure old Daddy won't mind.'

4 Remember that divorce isn't the only way of resolving a marriage breakdown. You can also drain the joint account and flee to a villa on a small Greek island.

5 'Ancillary relief' is a term for the possible financial orders that a court can make. It does not refer to your husband's activities with the co-respondent, aka 'that bitch'.

6 Divorce will have a huge impact on your relationships with mutual friends. Why not draw up a list to determine which of you 'gets' whom? You'll both stake a claim on the most dysfunctional ones because neither of you will be able to bear being around smug happy families. Indeed, when friends admit to having marital problems or complicated step-families you'll be so relieved you may well collapse.

7 Immediately after the separation, it's natural to experience feelings of intense loss similar to grief. These can be kept in check by regular ingestion of a 'cheeky Lemsip': the juice of two lemons combined with three ground-up Xanax tablets, two ground-up Nurofen Plus and a large measure of good quality single malt whisky.

8 Once you announce your intention to separate, expect to be on a rollercoaster that costs a minimum of 10K a ticket and lasts at least two years. And you feel sick for the entire ride.

9 Afterwards, make sure you hide all the court documents securely away from the kids' prying eyes. They don't need to know that Daddy was into bondage porn.

THINGS YOU COULD (PROBABLY) BUY WITH THE MONEY YOU'D THROW AWAY GETTING DIVORCED

14 Ford Focus 1.6 Estates (2004 reg)

+

23,000 EAT Coconut & Raspberry Slices

+

8,234 Ingmar Bergman DVD box sets

+

1 two-bedroom flat in Holland Park

+

15,427 copies of *We Need To Talk About Kevin* by Lionel Shriver

Divorce Menu

Starter: Revenge (served cold)

*

Main course: Humble pie
(with side order of baked beans
heated on Baby Belling stove in bedsit)

*

Washed down with: Tears

COUGARS AND SUGAR DADDIES

Older women dating younger men

Role models: Madonna, Samantha from *Sex and the City*, Courteney Cox in *Cougar Town*, Joan Collins.

Why: there aren't any single men your own age as they are all dating younger women.

Where to find love: toyboywarehouse.com; grown-up son's friends; your seminar group; supermarket; small ads, and actually just leaving the house after dark and going to places where other grown-ups may be gathering.

What makes you attractive to younger men: you have your own place; can cook; don't put him under pressure to have children (you've either already been there or never wanted to go there in the first place); you know what you want and are too busy to play games; years of yoga have made you eye-poppingly flexible.

What's in it for you: he doesn't have to be mothered through a midlife crisis; has been out recently enough to still know where to go; no baggage; experimental; doesn't talk about his prostate at dinner; pert buttocks; stamina.

Older men dating younger women

Role models: the Middle-Aged Guys from *The Fast Show*, Rod Stewart, Woody Allen, Tony Curtis, Paul Daniels.

Why: men possess an evolutionary urge to seek out a fertile mate likely to reproduce, but really you just want to fulfil a common male fantasy and make your friends sick with jealousy.

Where to find love: your seminar group; the office; walking your dog; private gym; weddings; catalogues. Do not attempt to chat up groups of young women in a bar – you will look sad.

What makes you attractive to younger women: your stimulating conversation; you have your own transport; you're patient, mature, protective; you may already have demonstrated your fertility; money.

What's in it for you: she's too young to realise you don't actually know what you're talking about; pert breasts; peer envy.

- -

SEPARATE BEDS

Don't suffer in silence – or indeed, the opposite of silence. Go single!

Remember, when you were younger (and, in fairness, thinner), you thought nothing of sharing a single bed with someone. The mere promise of proximity to another person's body was so thrilling that it banished all thoughts of discomfort and sleeplessness. Sure, you could see there might be benefits to having a bigger bed. But you were 19, so these were mostly to do with sex.

The first thing you did upon moving in with your partner was go to IKEA and buy a big bed. And for a while it was blissful. But then three things happened. One: your partner started snoring. Two: your partner started writhing and wriggling and, occasionally, shouting out gibberish in the middle of the night. Three: you had children and so became used to the phenomenon of not being able to get back to sleep after getting up to attend to them. 'I can't sleep.' 'Yes you can. Just relax.' 'I still can't sleep.' 'Calm down, for fuck's sake. It's 3.32.' 'You're making me tense.' 'I'm making you tense?' etc etc.

Separate beds were the obvious solution, but you worried, understandably, about the social stigma. *People will think we don't have sex any more. And it's true, we don't. But we don't want to be explicit about it.* Then you read an article in what you're still calling a 'newspaper' which made you feel better. A survey by the National Sleep Foundation in 2001 found that 12% of married Americans were sleeping alone. By 2005, this figure had risen to 23%.

You tried this information out the next time you had friends round for dinner and were surprised by how well it went down; by how interested everyone was; by how *enthusiastically* they nodded when you said you'd send them the link. It reassured you, and hardly anything does that these days.

Of course, posh people in history have always had two master bedrooms. (Your National Trust excursions should have taught you that.) The Queen and Prince Philip have long slept in separate beds – and *there's* a relationship to aspire to!

- -

Sally: … and I'm gonna be 40.
Harry: When?
Sally: Someday.
Harry: In eight years!
Sally: But it's there. It's just sitting there, like some big dead end. And it's not the same for men. Charlie Chaplin had kids when he was 73.
Harry: Yeah, but he was too old to pick them up.

'When Harry Met Sally' (1989)

This adequate two-bedroom pebbledash flat on the wrong side of the tracks isn't really two-thirds of the price of the light-filled Victorian family home that we're selling for you far too cheaply, is it?

SITTING ROOM: will accommodate the shit spare-room telly; sofa stand-in bean bags; and approx 156 sq ft of pain. Recesses: infinite.

MASTER BEDROOM: we know you didn't leave your male oppressor to get a chamber named after him, but you can't mess with years of estate agent archaisms.

BEDROOM 2: would fit a divorce-regulation mock-pine IKEA bunk bed. Construction: see series 2, episode 4 of The Wire when Jimmy McNulty tries to build his before his children arrive.

BATHROOM: look on the bright side. Oh, there isn't one? Windows are overrated. Anyway, who's going to phone the window cleaner now?

ATTIC: lots of storage space for repressed memories of your parents' own traumatic divorce, especially the time your mother encouraged you to keep a note of your father's phone conversations when you were staying with him.

GARDEN: 30 sq ft of cement. We noticed that when you brought your lover round to view (yuck! Much preferred your husband! Did you really think we believed it was your 'brother'?) he was asking if there would be room for a 'kids' tree house' in the garden. Don't worry, we're sure he'll love them!

MIDLIFE HERO:

DCS Foyle from *Foyle's War*

Detective Chief Superintendent Christopher Foyle was born in 1893. He fought in the trenches and married several months before the armistice in early 1918. His wife, Rosalind, died in 1932. So Foyle was 46 when the Second World War began – a fine age. Did we mention he brought up their son, Andrew, all by himself? Well, we're mentioning it now.

Foyle's 'beat' is Hastings. (You should go there, it's nice – apart from Warrior Square, which smells of wee.) He can drive but chooses not to because he wants Honeysuckle Weeks to drive him instead. This is because he likes the way she drives – the way she kicks down on the accelerator pedal with her heavy black boots; turns the steering wheel with a great sweep of her Land Girl arms; sings 'Tomorrow Belongs To Me' in a lusty contralto while shaking her hair free of its simple metal clips so that it CASCADES like a waterfall down her slender (but not too slender) khaki shoulders.

6.
IN OFFICE HOURS

Once, you had ambition. You were going to rise through the ranks and, when you reached the top, transform your company! But it hasn't happened like that. The world changed without telling you first, and now there are hordes of interns happy to do your job for nothing – assuming, that is, you still have a job. Wouldn't it be better just to live in the middle of the countryside and make chutney?

THE POINT OF WORK BY THE TIME YOU GET TO MIDLIFE

Earning money: 95%

Bantering with co-workers: 47%

Fulfilling personal ambitions: 8%

Learning new skills: 11%

Intellectual stimulation: 21%

As a distraction from the certainty of death: 80%

Contributing to the sum of human happiness: 7%

Contributing something meaningful and lasting to society: 12%

Making your children proud of you: 3%

Acquiring work-related ailments (asthma, RSI, cancer, etc): 74%

LATE DEVELOPERS

It's always reassuring to read about people who discovered their talents late in life, by which we mean 'when they were older than you'. Bill Gates founded Microsoft when he was seven, or something. But let's not worry about him. Let's celebrate, instead, the likes of....

Liz Smith: top actress, you've seen her in loads of things, usually playing batty grandmothers. She didn't start acting professionally until she was 50.

Colonel Sanders: at 40, he was a chef in a humble Kentucky service station. Then, when he was in his sixties, he founded Kentucky Fried Chicken. Thanks, Colonel.

Leos Janacek: Czech composer, didn't achieve success until 1904 when, at the age of 50, he wrote *Jenufa*.

Joshua Millner: was 61 when he won a gold medal in free rifle, 1,000 yards at the 1908 Olympics. He also finished ninth in the 'single shot running deer' event. Seriously – he did, and there was one.

Mary Wesley: the author of *The Camomile Lawn* published her first novel at 70. Have you read it? You should do; it's quite saucy.

Michael Haneke: the director of audience-baiting middle-class guiltfest *Hidden* didn't make a film until he was 47. He kept his talents 'hidden' all that time, ha ha ha ha ha ha ha!!!

Vaclav Havel: became President of Czechoslovakia at 53, though admittedly he was quite a successful playwright before then. (There's Ronald Reagan, too – Governor of California at 55, US President at 69 – but there we leave the celebrations.)

Frank Skinner: was 34 when he won the Perrier Award at the Edinburgh Fringe in 1991. Actually, that's quite young, isn't it? Maybe forget about him.

Anita Roddick: was also 34 when she founded The Body Shop in 1976. Look, for the purposes of this box, 34 is old, okay?

Charles, Prince of Wales: in his early sixties and is he king yet? No.

- -

PENSIONZZZZZZZ...

This accidental oversight is probably more common for people in creative or casualised professions, home workers and the self-employed than for those who joined a company on the milk round and stuck with it. But as the former are a demographic trend, and most of the latter have probably been made redundant by now, the subject has a broad enough relevance to be addressed here.

Part of the reason you don't have a pension is probably because all that talk of annuities and stakeholders seemed far too boring. And there's something rather demeaning about being patronised by an adolescent in a badly fitting suit drawing you graphs and telling you your whole family will die in poverty unless you buy his financial product – and it'll *all be your fault.*

In fact, an alarming (or reassuring, depending on how you look at it) 2.5 million people in the UK don't have a pension. Should you panic?

The rule of thumb trotted out by financial advisers is that, to work out how much you should be contributing to a pension each month, you halve the age at which you started your pension, and use this as a percentage of your gross salary.

According to thisismoney.co.uk, 'Assuming growth of 7% a year, savers must put away 1.5% of earnings every year for 40 years to be able to retire with just 50% of final salary.' And the *Guardian's* ready reckoner reckons that even people who are 35–40, looking to retire at 65 and hoping to have a pension of around £15,000 a year, need to start contributing £500 a month. Now.

Those of you who've been making National Insurance contributions will be in line for a state pension if you keep it up for more than 30 years; if you retired today, that would see you living off £97.65 a week. So let's hope you've cleared that mortgage and credit card backlog by then.

The good news is, it's probably a waste of time to panic. Pension funds have been going down the toilet anyway. Pension income fell 72% between 2000 and 2010. Better to spend any spare cash on something you enjoy, like wine, or art, or property. Or lottery tickets.

Incidentally, you've got a one in six chance of dying before 65 anyway (with men twice as likely to kick the bucket as women). Imagine if you'd spent all those years paying into a pension and then that happens. Bummer.

'The first sign of maturity is the discovery that the volume knob also turns to the left.'

Jerry M Wright

'IT'S NOT THAT WE WANT TO LOSE YOU...'

Midlife tends to be when redundancy strikes... and it can feel awful, like the beginning of the end of your ability to make money and be a useful member of society. But consider the facts and it quickly starts to seem less like a slate that's fallen off the roof of the universe onto your head and more like a .... well, er, an inevitable rite of passage.

Do:
• network like mad in pursuit of work. Really embarrass yourself. Change your personality if you have to.
• take up as many hobbies and evening classes as possible. You never know: the person sitting next to you in woodwork may have an uncle who needs a cleaner...
• use redundancy as an excuse to go into therapy.

Don't:
• use therapy – and the buried trauma it uncovered and linked back to that time you were trampled by a donkey when you were eight – as an excuse not to look for work.
• sneak back into your former workplace dressed as a lift engineer but with a rat in your pocket.

And definitely don't:
• get into the habit of 'nipping to the pub for lunch'.

TIME TO RELAX...

The bad news is that retirement is some way off for you – and realistically, by the time it has you in its cosy clutches, you'll be too frail to enjoy it. But the good news is that you can still dream...

Top ten retirement fantasies

Orient Express: the proper London-to-Venice job, not the one where you putter through the Hampshire countryside drinking tea and pointing at sheep.

Cruise: a classy one with famous lecturers and a 'country-house-style' library, though it mustn't berth – is that a verb? – at any country where 'funny food' is served.

Writing a novel: everyone has one novel in them. Barbara Cartland had 723. Well, sort of...

Move to a foreign country: though not one where there is 'funny food', etc.

Get a dog: but not a boundy one that will knock you over when you become frail – a dog is for life, not just for your late fifties.

Bake more: Once you're on statins, you can eat as much stodge as you like.

Rethink your look: Or don't – silver hair is in right now. Explains style icon Pixie Geldof: 'I didn't want to do another colour like pink, grey just seemed obvious.' You see?

Get a new car: An automatic – gears are hard on arthritic hands.

Catch up on culture: 'What was that film called? The one about Queen Victoria when she was young? It's on the tip of my tongue...'*

Get more involved in the local community: 'Sally *said* she'd baked the shortbread herself, but anyone could see it was from Sainsbury's...'

And The Reality...

Work: because it never ends.

Poverty: because your pension will be worthless.

Illness: waits for you to retire, then pounces like a randy panther.

Care home: 'spacious en-suite rooms', 'quality home-cooked food', 'tranquil location', etc.

* *The Young Victoria*

**'Is that a birthday? 'tis, alas! too clear;
'Tis but the funeral of the former year.
'Tis but the funeral of the former year.'**

Alexander Pope

Q. Hello, hello. I can see you're busy so I won't keep you long. Gosh, your desk is messy! You must have worked here for years! When I was at uni I...

A. Will you get to the point, please?

Q. Of course, sorry, sorry. Um, I had a question? Is a company a meritocracy if it's staffed by people who are only there because they're either cheap or not being paid at all?

A. No. Companies aren't meritocracies. That isn't how late capitalism works.

Q. Great, thanks. I thought as much. By the way, Nicola in HR wants to see you...

CHUTNEY FANTASIES

'Chutney fantasy' is a generic term for escape-route dreams, many of which genuinely involve the dramatic quitting of a job in order to forge a new career making artisanal chutney over open fires in copper pans reclaimed from National Trust properties.

Typically, it takes root shortly after the onset of midlife, growing and growing until suddenly you're phoning up banks to ask about business development loans. 'It will be really special chutney,' you say. 'Pear and ginger, but with prunes too. We've got this idea for specially shaped jars, a bit like that St Peter's Ale which comes in replica 18th-century beer bottles.' You explain that it will be a premium product, designed to be sold in the sort of delis where people won't mind paying £6.95 a jar. Yes, it is a lot, but start-up costs will be high. And obviously you'll be paying yourself the salary you were on when you were doing crisis PR for Tesco.

Other popular chutney fantasies include:
• Opening a B&B, but a really good one. 'People get it so wrong. The trick is making sure the sausages you serve at breakfast have a high pork content – nothing less than 75% will do.'
• Writing songs. 'I'm 48 so pop-stardom is no longer a realistic goal for me. But professional songwriting – that's a piece of piss. If I spend an hour mucking about on GarageBand and drop a CD off at EMI Music Publishing this afternoon, I bet you they'll have got back to me before the week's out to say Cheryl wants the track for her new album...'
• Landscape gardening. 'I read this great biography of Capability Brown. He was amazing, the way he tamed unruly nature, moving trees around and stuff. I could do that. And I've found these great "gardening" trousers on the Jigsaw website.'
• Teaching. 'I know people say teaching's hard, but it can't be harder than managing the supply chain at a small Leeds-based manufacturer of burglar-alarm components – and I've done that for 15 years! It's time to put something *back*... Kids just need to be inspired and reassured that they can *really do something* with their lives.'
• Starting a greetings card business. 'People are looking for something different, something tasteful. But cheerful, too. I could use fun images like cupcakes and buttons. I always felt I was artistic, but I've never found the right outlet. I thought I could sell these online. They'd be ever so popular – especially with the other NCT mums.'

- Photography, 'I took some great shots of the local landscape last time we went to Crete. Everyone said what a good eye I've got. Hey, here's an idea – I could *have them transferred to canvas* and sell them as art prints!'
- Setting up a market stall. 'Selling pretty knitted things. Or handmade jewellery – I learnt how to do it on that weekend course at our local art gallery. It might be a bit chilly in winter, but the other day I saw this really cool retro Citroën van for sale. We could convert it and take it round festivals selling proper coffee! And gourmet pies! And that artisanal chutney my mate makes!'

'Middle life is the moment of greatest unfolding, when a man still gives himself to his work with his whole strength and his whole will. But in this very moment evening is born, and the second half of life begins. Passion now changes her face and is called duty; I want becomes the inexorable I must and the turnings of the pathway that once brought surprise and discovery become dulled by custom.'

Carl Jung

7.
OCCUPATIONAL THERAPY

Midlife is so tiring, you need all the idle distractions you can find. Why not dignify this weird cluster of activities by referring to them as 'hobbies'? It works for us.

BLOGGING

Midlife is the time when you discover you have lots of opinions on topics you never knew you cared about. That café, for instance – the one that's opening down the road. It used to be a horrible takeaway which everyone hated. But the new owners have really screwed up. They've thrown away all their local 'goodwill' credits by installing a red aluminium shopfront that's so ugly it might as well be made of uPVC. Now, wood is expensive, you realise that. But there must have been other options. What about a silver anodised finish? That would have looked so much less... downmarket.

You'd make your feelings known in person, but the last time you passed the café there was no one there. At least, the *owners* didn't seem to be there. The builders were. They were burly and shaven-headed and (you thought) Polish and, well, what with the language difficulty there was bound to be, it didn't seem worth interrupting them to make what they might misconstrue as a rude, busybodyish observation.

It was then that you had the idea for your blog – an outlet for your thoughts about 'local issues' to be called something light-hearted and amusing. What the community needs more than anything is someone like you making the sort of observations others are too scared to make, even Richard Littlejohn.

Because look: the whole area is going to the dogs. Have you seen the kids from St Horatio's walking home? The way they chuck burger wrappers on the ground and hit each other with sticks and shout shout shout as if the most important thing in the world is that we all hear the asinine fucking rubbish that passes for conversation between 16-year-olds these days?

- -

JOINING A BOOK GROUP

How nice to read a book and sit around talking about it with like-minded people. So grown-up! Typically, Julie hosts. You sit in her kitchen drinking wine and eating cheese and... it's nice.

No, fine.

No, nice. Nice is the word.

What's the problem? Well, if we're being honest, Julie is a bit on the controlling side. A bit of a school swot. (She used to be a teacher but quit after her nervous breakdown – the nervous breakdown *that must never be mentioned*.) And she always press-gangs everyone into choosing the same sort of book: either those Richard & Judy novels in which timorous ingénues find caches of letters in attics or what she calls 'acknowledged modern classics' like sodding *White Teeth* or arsing *Life of Pi* or sodding, arsing *Birdsong*.

So a couple of weeks ago, you suggested the group read *The Echoing Grove* by Rosamond Lehmann, not because you're some pompous literary twat but because, well, it's brilliant and underrated.

'There was a film of *The Echoing Grove*, you pointed out, hoping it would sway her. 'It was called *The Heart of Me*. Helena Bonham Carter was in it.'

'Oh,' said Julie. 'I saw that. It was really depressing.'

'Well, yes.'

'It was all about divorce and betrayal. The characters weren't very sympathetic.'

'Well, no.'

'I think we should do *The Lovely Bones*.'

What you wanted to say: 'What could be more depressing and unsympathetic than an "inspirational" novel about a 14-year-old girl being murdered? WHAT?'

What you actually said: 'Okay.'

- -

MAKING BREAD (IN A BREADMAKER)

It's natural, as you get older, to hark back to the way things were done in the old days, ie properly. So you nodded vigorously upon reading that the Real Bread Campaign had condemned supermarkets' bakery sections as 'tanning salons' where loaves made and part-cooked earlier were browned off. The RBC, as you're now calling it, said customers were victims of 'legalised deception' and that supermarkets were guilty of practising 'retail theatre'.

So! You won't be buying that squishy-crusty French artisanal loaf from Sainsbury's again. Because you'll be making your own! In a breadmaker. A Panasonic, because they invented them in the mid-'80s and it's important to be loyal to the companies that invent things. (For this reason, you only ever bought JVC videos.)

Is it true that all breadmakers do is mimic industrial bread-making processes? Of course it is, but we won't dwell on that here.

MIDLIFE CLINIC: **CARS**

Q. What car should I be driving? I've seen a nice red Ferrari Testarossa...

A. No, no, no! Nothing says midlife crisis louder.

Q. You haven't answered my question. What car should...

A. Just wait! We're doing research! Machines are humming. Oompa-loompas are flicking through index cards. Right, here we are: a survey conducted by Green Mile (2007) found men between 35 and 45 would choose to drive the following if money were no object:

1 Porsche Boxster
2 Audi TT
3 Range Rover Sport
4 Porsche 911
5 Honda S2000
6 Subaru Impreza
7 VW Golf GTI
8 BMW X5
9 Lotus Elise
10 Nissan 350Z

Q. No people movers, I see! [Clarkson face.]

A. Well, no. No one *wants* to get a people mover. They're the thermal underwear of motoring. But if you took a series of decisions in your twenties and thirties that have led you to a point where you have children then you're doomed to spend some time behind the wheel of a 'family car'. The good news is that, beyond 60, driving a sports car, especially something vintage, is more likely to be seen as the mark of someone with an interesting hobby rather than a cupboard stuffed with poppers and Viagra. Plus, you'll have a free bus pass to help you get around when it breaks down.

KEEPING CHICKENS

Ever since you stayed in that farmhouse B&B, you've thought how lovely it would be to have fresh eggs for breakfast every morning. And even though you never did move to the countryside and start your own farm, you can fool yourself that you did by installing a hen coop in your back garden, buying a pair of bantams, giving them amusing names (Torville & Dean, Vita & Virginia, Andy & Vince), then watching a few old episodes of *The Good Life* for tips. As with children, there is also the opportunity to acquire designer accessories such as the Eglu – the Bugaboo of chicken coops.

An important factor in deciding to keep chickens is the extra income you'll be able to make by writing about them in what we persist in calling 'newspaper colour supplements': how you've decided to let them forage on pasture rather than give them industrial feed because it results in healthier eggs; and how, when you got bored with them, you simply flapped them into the back of the Focus, drove to the Hanger Lane gyratory and released them into the traffic cooing, 'Go, little birds, go!'

Okay, maybe not that.

DETOXING

Midlife hangovers are so shockingly violent you think only drastic action will curb the turmoil in your head and stomach and liver and gall bladder. So you go online and find an appropriately austere regime. Well, not *too* austere. You draw the line at birch tea. What about 'semi-fasting' for three days on a mixture of fruit and vegetables with vitamins and herbal drinks? That sounds do-able. Oh, hang on – wholemeal rice. It recommends wholemeal rice. You're not eating that; haven't eaten it since 1991. And thistle! Yuck. That's almost as bad as birch. On the plus side, you're allowed porridge with two teaspoons of honey or golden syrup for breakfast because – it says here – oats (*Avena sativa*) are a herb which act as a gentle sedative and nerve rebuilder. Well. You never knew *that*. Though to be fair, you never knew a lot of things, like how to ask, 'What's in this cocktail, exactly?'

How long before you can start drinking again? Let's see... Six weeks. SIX WEEKS! No way...

- -

DIY

That picture's crooked.

- -

EMBROIDERY

On the one hand, personalised gifts are a lovely gesture. Sewing is therapeutic, and a good way to give up smoking. These days it's even considered okay to sew in clubs.

On the other, are a tea towel embroidered with pictures of fruit or an appliquéd egg cosy really necessary in life?

- -

WONDERING WHICH GADGETS TO BUY

What you really want, right, what you *really* want is a transformative device. It might be an iPad or the very latest iPhone, not a crappy old 3GS, who wants one of those? It might be a Roberts iPod docking station in shiny piano-key black' or one of those Sony things that lets you stream songs wirelessly from your computer all round the house. Or it might be something in the kitchen, like a coffee machine that uses pods. You get a box of pods, with tasting notes – that's £15 well spent.

Gadgets are nature's way of demonstrating how much the world has improved in the course of your lifetime. Everything is getting simpler and easier. Remember how excited your grandfather was to get his hands on an 8mm cine camera? After war and austerity, home movies! He would have loved the internet; would have wept with joy at the very thought of Asda Online. But sadly, he died in 1977. He never got to see a Walkman, let alone the latest range of very, very cheap children's clothes – stitched by tiny hands for ever bigger people.

What developments will we miss? All the good ones. Nano-bikes for ants, that sort of thing.

The best gadgets are often the ones furthest from the bleeding edge of technological innovation. Like Breville Sandwich Toasters. The other day, your therapist asked you what you really wanted out of life and you said, 'A toasted cheese and ham sandwich.' You explained that when you were young you really wanted a Breville Sandwich Toaster, but your mother said, 'No, we've just bought a Soda Stream because you asked for one. What do you think we are, made of money?'

You reminded your therapist about the early-'80s advert for Breville Sandwich Toasters which showed a sandwich weeping in the fridge because it didn't like being cold. The tagline was: 'Don't be mingy, help a sandwich.'

You couldn't say 'mingy' in an advert now. Well, you could, but only on those special channels that Daddy watches when he's feeling a bit sad.

- -

GAMBLING

Somehow your life hasn't turned out to be as thrilling or as lucrative as you'd envisaged. So you gamble. Even a little flutter gets the adrenalin going. Maybe you start small, putting a fiver on the Grand National, playing the National Lottery 'because it's just like giving to charity'. Maybe you win. It makes you happy. Maybe you lose, but at least you were emotionally engaged with something, and that felt good. The next thing you know you'll be sitting in front of the slot machines in Blackpool with a bucket of change and leopard-print leggings. Keep that vision in mind whenever it threatens to become an addiction, and remember that the odds of getting all six numbers in the National Lottery are $49!/(6!*(49-6)!)$, ie 1 in 13,983,816, ie really not very likely at all.

- -

MAKING YOUR OWN STOCK

It tastes so much better, doesn't it? *Doesn't* it?

Who knows when or how it starts? Perhaps you're in a meeting, daydreaming of a better life – a life where you've got so much time and energy left over after clearing up Sunday lunch that it's really no trouble, no trouble at all, to start chopping up *more* fucking onions and carrots and parsnips? Or perhaps your children are small and you've decided to make your own stock because bought stock (ie stock cubes and the ridiculously expensive ready-made stock you find in upmarket delis) has too much salt in it?

No one would deny it's an enjoyable business, for a bit. There you stand at the hob, inhaling the delicious steam, amazed at how easy it is, this stock-making malarkey. You feel… empowered. You might as well be at River Cottage, spearing fish and wrestling pigs. Almost certainly, you are more attractive to the opposite sex when making stock than when not.

Experts call what follows the Two-Month Stock Honeymoon Period (TMSHP). For two months, give or take a few days, you go stock crazy. Become a stock bore. People want to sell you on the stock exchange, ha ha.

To the children: 'Hey, don't throw that half-eaten carrot away, I can put it in the stock.'

To your partner: 'I say, there's a good "stock" of stock in the freezer.'

To the butcher: 'Oh hi, hi. I'd like a chicken please, that big one… but can I have the giblets too because [warm glow of pride suffuses face] I WANT TO MAKE SOME STOCK?'

Is this how people used to cook? Is it how your *parents* used to cook? No. They would have thought, if they thought about it at all, that making stock was a waste of time and, moreover, French. (No one in Britain in the 1960s and '70s made stock. They were too busy watching the *Morecambe and Wise Christmas Special* and trying to get their cars to start.) What's the point of microwaveable plastic if you're going to make stock? Didn't Birds Eye invent their Steakhouse range of grills so that people *never had to do things like make stock again*?

Traditionally, stock manufacture reverts to Once Or Twice A Year (OOTAY) at the end of the TMSHP.

- -

GARDENING

Psssst – the lawn needs mowing. No, it's your turn…

SORTING CDS

They won't organise themselves, you know.

Consider, please, the vast stretches of prime shelf space given over to CDs you haven't played for years. You need to cull. It's the only way. A tip: you may find you don't need to be as ruthless as all that. It's not about ruthlessness, it's about... self-selection. What are we trying to say? Well, look... that Turin Brakes album, the one you bought because you liked that strummy one about having WD40 in your veins – you don't even need to think about that, do you? Or the second Dandy Warhols album. Or that Elvis Costello album with the string quartet. Christ, it was dull. And why do you have the Aqua album? It hasn't really stood the test of time, has it? Wasn't quite the 'post-ironic Europop masterpiece' you declared it to be back in 1997 as you were sipping post-ironic absinthe out of post-ironic Charles & Di mugs (she'd just died) in that flat in Tulse Hill where you were kept awake by roosting pigeons. So: in the bin – now, please. Yes, you can feed 'Barbie Girl' into iTunes first.

What's that you say? You don't want to throw them away? You just want to pass the time of day organising them according to some random principle? You should have said! Though you know you're just rearranging deckchairs on the Titanic, don't you?

'An archaeologist is the best husband any woman can have: the older she gets, the more interested he is in her.'

Agatha Christie

WONDERING WHAT KATE BUSH IS UP TO

Making a new record? Cutting her toenails? Making a record *while* cutting her toenails?

MIDLIFE CONUNDRUM: **CAN I STILL LEARN TO PLAY A MUSICAL INSTRUMENT?**

Or perhaps what you really mean is: Can I be a rock star in my forties?

It came free with the paper today – a guide to playing 'riffs' from famous songs by AC/DC and The Who. Inspired by the photo of Pete Townshend windmilling his arms, you went straight up to the attic and dug out the electric guitar and practice amp you bought 20 years ago when you were going to be a pop star. Now, now: don't flinch – you were. You had it all worked out! The gimmick was that you and your friend Martin were a synthesizer duo, *but with guitars*. You were called Par Avion and the plan was to dress up as pilots (or was it postmen?) on *Top of the Pops*. You made a demo on a four-track machine Martin bought at a car-boot sale, but when you played it to people they… well, they didn't dance, they made a face as if you'd shown them pictures of their grandparents wearing gimp masks. At the time, you took this rejection on the chin; but it's needled and nagged and gnawed at you ever since. Why didn't they love it? Why didn't they love it *when there was so much to love*? Only recently has the answer become clear: you couldn't play the guitar. At all. I mean, you couldn't write songs either, but let's focus on the guitar thing for now.

To become really good at something – or, in your case, not fist-chewingly terrible at something – you have to learn to do it when you're young and practise a lot. (There's a whole book about this: *Outliers* by Malcolm Gladwell.) And while it would be cruel to call midlife a time for refining talents you possess rather than divining for ones you probably don't, it wouldn't be inaccurate either.

What about painting landscapes? You were quite good at that. Your art teacher compared you favourably to Prince Charles.

- -

NATIONAL TRUST

As a child, you thought the countryside was boring. In your twenties, you thought it was a Thomas Hardy theme park. Only in midlife do you start to appreciate how amazing it is, and how nice it might be to preserve it for the benefit of the nation. This is where National Trust membership comes in.

Of course, your clever-clever teenage children will laugh at you for taking it out. You will rebuke them sternly and quote Simon Jenkins to the effect that houses like those owned and managed by the Trust are a 'conversation between beauty and utility down the ages': 'Through them we hear the echo of our collective selves – and remember who we are.'

They will say yes, that's all very well, but it doesn't explain why all NT houses look kind of the same.

They don't, you say.

They do, they say, because the point of the exercise is to close up the financial and ideological gulf between you and the people who once lived in them so you don't come away feeling alienated.

That's not the point of the exercise, you say. And stop lecturing me on the iniquities of the heritage industry, you in your Pink Floyd T-shirt. The point of the exercise is...

There is a pause. What? say your children.

Charity, you say. And jam. Damson jam.

How to get the most out of visiting National Trust properties
1 Mug up on the history of the house before you go.
2 Go to the shop first or you will spend the whole visit dreaming of 'Music That Won The War' CDs and lavender eye-masks. Resist the temptation to buy the National Trust version of Monopoly. It's a good gag, but at £25 an expensive one.
3 Save the teashop till last or you will end up going twice – and at your age your body can only tolerate so much millionaire's shortbread.
4 Leave any teenage children at home. They'll only mope around and keep asking sarcastically if there's a ghost.
5 Bring a Farrow & Ball swatch with you for easy reference.
6 Be nice to the volunteers. Ask them stuff. They like that.

'Grow old with me!
The best is yet to be.'

Robert Browning, 'Rabbi Ben Ezra'

OBITUARIES

It used to be that you reacted to the death of a famous figure with incredulity. 'I didn't even realise they were still alive,' you'd remark.

Nowadays, you still react with incredulity, but along the lines of 'Him? But X can't have been much older than 50!' Followed by even greater incredulity when you realise that, although X was indeed in his fifties when he made all those movies, that was at least 20 years ago *for both of you*.

You have even taken to glancing cursorily at the obituaries of people you have never heard of. Not so much to find out about their many and varied achievements, nor to read the touching tributes from their peers, but to find out *how old they were and what they died of.*

POKER

Playing poker on a Friday night with your mates is a fun way to keep in touch with university friends and colleagues from your last job but one. What it's not is a Bond film. Just because you string together incomprehensible sentences using terms like flop, river and big blind and drink home-made martinis does not mean you are a secret agent or East End gangster. Face it: the closest you're going to get to living dangerously is asking for extra jalapeño on the pizza you call out for around eleven.

SHEDS

'Shed' is a metaphor for 'male space'. It doesn't have to be a shed. It could be an attic. Though not a cellar. That would have different, frankly Viennese connotations and we're already struggling to make the shed/attic thing sound humdrum, inevitable, unthreatening when what we're really thinking of is Aston in Pinter's *The Caretaker*.

The shed is the chrysalis in which the midlife male encases himself. In butterflies, the chrysalis stage is characterised by little movement, though some pupae can move their abdomens to produce sounds or scare away predators. Similarly, men are able, within the cramped confines of their sheds, to move their fingers on a remote control to shift between Sky Sports channels, Dave and BBC4 when it's having one of its hairy-men-playing-guitars-on-*Whistle Test* themed nights. Within the chrysalis, metamorphosis occurs: 'midlife' man undergoes a series of physical changes − puckering nipples, expanding ears − to emerge an 'old' man with a variety of robust views on inheritance tax, the benefits of uPVC windows and Lady Gaga.

The midlife woman prefers rooms to sheds and, when asked why, will typically respond: 'Look, Virginia Woolf didn't write *A Shed of One's Own*, did she? DID SHE?'

Top five male writers who liked to write books in their sheds

Roald Dahl
Dylan Thomas
George Bernard Shaw
Daphne du Maurier*
Philip Pullman

*Okay, okay, she wasn't a man.

> **'The old believe everything, the middle-aged suspect everything, the young know everything.'**
>
> Oscar Wilde

WALKING

'When my legs begin to move, my thoughts begin to flow,' declared the American writer and philosopher Henry David Thoreau. There's truth in this, plenty of it; though we'll draw a veil for now over Thoreau's death from bronchitis at 44. (His last words were: 'Now comes good sailing... moose... Indian.'). Also the fact that he contracted this bronchitis by walking in the rain in the middle of the night. (He was counting tree stumps.)

As we have seen, it's the midlifer's fate to find the modern world too fast. Walking slows it down, enabling us to notice things we didn't notice before. Not nasty things – not that new patch of graffiti on the side of the hut in the local park where the alcoholics hang out. But nice things. Things like, I don't know, badger setts. The sound of water as it trickles down the side of a mountain. Pebbles.

Walking is really good for you. Not, admittedly, as good for you as show-offy, jump-up-and-down aerobic exercise or jogging or something, but according to the British Heart Foundation, it has a 'high impact on cardiovascular disease', lowering blood pressure and cholesterol levels. The snag is that, for walking to have these benefits, you need to do it, briskly, for at least half an hour every day. There's an obvious joke waiting to be made here, but you can do it.

Essential midlife walking accessories
Portable defibrillator
Hip flask
Commode
Car (as back-up)
Good Pub Guide
Picnic set, including rug with waterproof backing
A stick
Actually, two sticks
A massive, unwieldy SLR camera which you'll spend the whole walk complaining about having to carry, as if bringing it was someone else's idea
An iPod containing rousing, symphonic film music, probably by John Barry, so that you can 'soundtrack' your walk
A pork pie
Actually, two pork pies

BUYING WINE FROM WINE MERCHANTS INSTEAD OF SUPERMARKETS

A good way to make yourself feel better about your reliance on booze is to start buying wine from a posh wine merchant. Suddenly, as if by magic, your incipient alcoholism is recast as an earnest drive to acquire oenological expertise. And it's so lovely, getting home of an evening to find a big, fat, glossy catalogue from Berry Bros & Rudd or Averys or The Wine Society sitting on the doormat, full of blather about 'peerless terroir' and 'cherry perfume and increasing silkiness on the palate' and photos of tubby, red-faced Cityboys bolting down £2,500 seven-course 'taster' dinners in the specially converted cellar.

Berry Bros is our favourite wine merchant because it has a royal warrant and was founded in 1698 by someone called the Widow Bourne, who we like to imagine as the great-great-great-great-great-great grandmother of frowny-faced action hero Jason Bourne. It used to be quite snooty and austere but has loosened up to the point where it was happy to let the cameras in for that BBC4 documentary you heard about but forgot to Sky+ last year. Not that you want looseness from a wine merchant, necessarily. But you know what we mean.

THE WI

Bear with us, please. The Women's Institute has come a long way since your mother's time. It's even come a long way since that film with Julie Walters and Helen Mirren posing naked except for a well-placed bun. Its original purpose was 'to revitalise rural communities and to encourage women to become more involved in producing food during the First World War'; now it's an excuse for a girls' night out and reconnecting with your crafty side after a hard day at the office – as likely to be found in Clapham as Ceredigion. Members still sew and make jam, but talks and demos are more often on belly-dancing and cocktail mixing than bee-keeping and perfect pruning. Talking of bee-keeping...

BEE-KEEPING

Bill Turnbull from *BBC Breakfast* keeps bees, as does *World at One* presenter Martha Kearney. But not together.

8.
I TOLD YOU I WAS ILL

If you're lucky, you'll have sustained only negligible wear and tear so far on your journey through life. But midlife is where it all changes – where it all starts to go horribly, horribly wrong. As ever, though, forewarned is forearmed. Think of yourself as going into battle like, er... those marines landing on Omaha Beach at the start of *Saving Private Ryan*. [Um, didn't they all get mown down by machine guns? – Ed]

Q. I seem to be getting fat all of a sudden. And yet throughout my twenties I hardly put any weight on at all. What's going on there?

A. You're eating too much and not exercising enough. Even if you're an ectomorph (ie naturally skinny type) who's never knowingly refused a scone, you'll still develop a spare tyre in your forties as your metabolism slows down and you lose muscle tone. After 45, you'll need to eat 200 fewer calories a day if you're to have a hope of maintaining your old weight. Avoid white bread and other refined foods, too. (You don't need to be told this, *do you? Do* you?) And do 30-45 minutes of aerobic exercise at least five times a week.

This means:
Running, cycling, lifting weights, playing football, swimming.

It does not mean:
Removing cork from bottle, reclining on sofa, crying.

THINGS THAT HELP YOU LIVE LONGER

Having a 'baby face'.
According to Danish scientists led by Professor Kaare Christensen of the University of Southern Denmark (*British Medical Journal*, 2009) who studied 387 pairs of twins and found that the younger-looking tended to live longer. This could be something to do with DNA influencing the speed at which cells can replicate. Or it could just be that a hard life tends to show in your face.

Living in Okinawa, Japan.
In a population of one million, 900 are centenarians. This is believed to be the result of a varied, fruit- and veg-heavy diet rich in antioxidants.

Living in Ovodda, Sardinia.
The only place where as many men reach 100 as women.

Having meetings that last for more than than 20 minutes.
Oh wait, that's right, actually it just *feels* like you're living longer.

'My own theory – or one of them – was that once you started to hit middle age, you became so jaded and unsurprised by life that you had to have a child in order to provide yourself with a new set of eyes through which to view things, to make them seem new and exciting again.'

Jonathan Coe, 'The Terrible Privacy of Maxwell Sim' (2010)

ALCOHOL

You don't want to hear this, but it's not very good for you and you should try to drink less of it. It makes you depressed, moody, tired, aggressive and bilious, and in midlife you're going to be feeling all these things anyway, so you don't need the situation aggravated. You don't want higher blood pressure, osteoporosis or mouth cancer. (These are all linked to excessive drinking.) Nor do you need to put on more weight – booze is incredibly calorific, plus it causes your blood sugar levels to crash leading to an overwhelming desire for curry and chips.

All of which said – and yes, it does seem to contradict what we've just urged above – a 1997 report by the American Cancer Society found that alcohol consumption 'was associated with a small reduction in the overall risk of death in middle age (ages 35 to 69)'. And (your favourite fact!) red wine contains flavonoids which possess antioxidant properties and aid the cardiovascular system.

MIDLIFE ILLNESSES

Midlife is when your mind and body start to give up on you. They've had enough, basically, and the fusillade of illnesses heading your way is, well... you know in 'Do They Know It's Christmas' there's that line about the only bells that ring in Africa being the 'clanging chimes of doom'? That's what these illnesses feel like (even when they're not, strictly speaking). Little tinkly bells rung by Mother Nature to say, 'Okay, time's nearly up – better make it clear in your will that you don't want "Angels" played at your funeral.'

- -

C*****

C***** happens when your cells get tired and decide they can no longer be bothered to divide properly. Instead, they divide in a chaotic, disorderly fashion which, were we to draw a glib comparison with writing, would be like us suddenly typing eusgufsugfsugfrgrgrgyysf and thinking that was okay, even funny. But it ISN'T.

Midlifers may find it easier to think of c***** in terms of the 1976 sci-fi film *Logan's Run*, about a sinister future society where everyone is exterminated at the age of 30 – a bit like working in arts journalism, ha ha. One man, Logan (Michael York), decides to avert his chosen destiny even though he's a 'sandman' whose job is to exterminate 'runners'. He flees the domed city where everyone now lives (and where for some reason there aren't any non-white people: maybe there's another dome round the corner that we can't see?) with sexy renegade Jessica (Jenny Agutter). But they're pursued by Logan's former friend and fellow sandman Francis. In the end they find the 'sanctuary' they crave, but it turns out to be a post-apocalyptic Washington DC in whose ruins an Old Man (Peter Ustinov) is living with a load of cats.

Plot this graphically and we end up with:

LOGAN = rogue c*****ous cell

JESSICA = oncogene (encourages c*****ous cells to multiply)

FRANCIS = tumour suppressor gene (stops cells multiplying)

OLD MAN = DNA repair gene (gene that repairs other damaged genes)

The good news: ten-year survival rates have gone up massively since the 1970s for the most common c*****s. The highest survival rates (calculated in May 2007) are for testicular c*****, malignant melanoma and Hodgkin's lymphoma. About the lowest survival rates we will say little except: stop smoking, now.

♥ disease

There are loads of different types of heart disease, all broadly similar in the sense that they end in the same way: with the heart conking out because the muscle has stopped working. Basically, you've got your:

• coronary heart disease: your arteries get clogged up with what scientists call 'goo';
• congestive heart failure: like having a nose that's so blocked up you can't breathe, except it's not your nose it's your heart;*
• hypertensive heart disease: when your blood pressure gets too high and your heart goes, 'Oooh, I don't like this, go a bit slower, I'm knackered';
• total eclipse of the heart: when you get a little bit tired of listening to the sound of your tears – and a little bit nervous that the best of all the years have gone by.

* *What do you think we are, experts?*

Hypochondria

By definition hypochondria, which reaches a peak in middle age, is an ongoing fear of illness based on the misinterpretation of physical symptoms or normal bodily functions. But realistically, *something's* going to be malfunctioning by the time you get to midlife. So how do you know you're misinterpreting? And why shouldn't you worry about it? Why shouldn't you go to the doctor every other day because you've found a lump under your arm? And that pins-and-needles feeling you keep getting when you're sitting at your desk. Sure, it could just be that you're sitting awkwardly. But what if it's Guillain-Barré syndrome, a rare nerve disorder which starts with pins and needles and progresses rapidly to muscle weakness and then paralysis and then needing a respirator to breathe and then... death?

HAVE YOU GOT DEMENTIA?

This is a version of the actual test that actual doctors use to diagnose dementia. Remember that bit in *Iris* (tagline: 'Her greatest gift was for life'*) when Iris Murdoch does the test and obviously it's not good, she's got Alzheimer's? *Do* you? Anyway.

Let a friend or family member administer this test or do it with a loved one. Score 1 point for each *wrong* answer and enter under **Errors**. Keep in mind the **maximum number of errors** for each question. Multiply the number of errors by the given weight. Then add each score to come to the final score.

Questions	Max. no. of errors	Errors Weight	Score
1. What year is it now?	1	x4=	
2. What month is it now?	1	x3=	
3. Repeat this memory phrase and try to remember it: "Can't you fold your clothes before you put them away like a normal person?"	4	x2=	
4. About what time is it now? (within 1 hour)	1	x3=	
5. Count backwards from 20 to 1	19	x2=	
6. Say the months in reverse order	7	x2=	
7. Repeat the memory phrase again	5	x2=	

Total: _____

*No it *fucking* wasn't. Her greatest gift was for writing 26 novels, 6 plays, 5 philosophical works and 2 collections of poetry

MINOR AGE-RELATED ILLNESSES WHICH ARE EXTREMELY COMMON AND WON'T KILL YOU, EVEN THOUGH THEY'RE EXTREMELY ANNOYING

• **Piles** – swollen veins in your arse. Don't pretend you don't know
• **Sebaceous hyperplasia** – tiny, acne-like pustules appear on your face for absolutely no good reason
• **Milia** – tiny, acne-like pustules appear on your face for absolutely no good reason
• **Macular degeneration** – you start going blind
• **Receding gums** – dentists can repair them using skin from the roof of your mouth
• **Hearing loss** – too much young persons' music!
• **Diverticulosis** – a disorder of the digestive tract
• **Constipation** — eat more prunes
• **Gallstones** – created as bile production slows
• **Itching** – often caused simply by dry, cracked skin

- -

MIDLIFE EXERCISE SPECIAL! PILATES

Hallo! I'm just off to the gym.

Oh good. Kettle bells? Spinning?

Pilates, actually. It's extremely popular with the over-35s. Gwyneth Paltrow does it.

Pilates isn't exercise. It's just licensed lying down. And how did Gwyneth Paltrow get to be over 35?

Actually, it's a lot harder that it looks. You have to hold your stomach in for a whole hour, without even wearing Spanx!

Yeah, yeah, I've seen that. It's lying on your side and lifting your leg off the ground by a centimetre while gripping a ball between your knees and listening to whale music. The most exciting it gets is when the teacher gets out the bag of giant rubber bands.

It's not about the bits you move, it's about keeping the rest of you still and balanced.

It's about not falling over?

Joseph Pilates (he invented it, by the way) called it Controlology: minimal movements aimed at strengthening the core muscles. It also promotes posterior lateral breathing.

Sorry?

Breathing into your ribcage.

So it's about lying down, breathing and not falling over?

In a nutshell, but you are actually using lots of muscles while you are doing it. Or not doing it. Or doing not doing it. Anyway... Pilates is designed to elongate and strengthen the body, while promoting mobility and muscle tone. It prevents osteoporosis, relieves stress, encourages good posture.

Yes, lovely. But what muscles would I be working?

External oblique, internal oblique, rectus abdominus, transvers abdominus, intercostals.

I've never heard of those.

Pelvic floor.

I've heard of that. No one can see my pelvic floor, though. What's the point in that being well toned?

It stops you weeing yourself involuntarily (which is going to be handy as you get older, or sooner if you've ever given birth). *And* Pilates works your lumber muscles, which would help that back pain you're always going on about. And it would sort out that knee injury.

What knee injury?

The one that's stopped you going to the gym for the past three years.

Oh, yes, that knee injury. Ouch! Ow! [Exits rubbing joint]

MIDLIFE EXERCISE SPECIAL! **RUNNING**

Running's good, isn't it, in a low-impact, got-to-start-somewhere sort of way. There's a park round the corner; you can run there. Lots of people do – they look as if they're enjoying it.

So what do you have to do? To run?

First, fill your iPod Shuffle with 'running songs'.* This could take a while – choosing the right songs is a serious business and mustn't be rushed. But it needs to be done first, and properly, or you won't be in the right frame of mind, and at this age it's all about frame of mind. What kit do you need? You can't use those old trainers, they're fucked. Get along to that new Intersport and treat yourself to a new pair. You can stock up on other running accoutrements while you're there: water bottles (you don't want to get dehydrated); socks; shorts; tops; tracksuit bottoms. (Is that what they're called nowadays?)

Do you wear shorts under the tracksuit bottoms like you did at school? And what do you wear under the shorts? Is there special underwear to stop, you know, *chafing*? (Isn't that what jockstraps were for?) The nice woman in Intersport will know. Actually, maybe it would be better to buy all this stuff online. Less embarrassing.

There's no shortage of websites selling running stuff. Look: tracksuit bottoms are now called 'long pants'. (Good job you didn't buy them in person.) Who knew running gear was so hi-tech? It's like cyclists' gear – all tight and stretchy and designed, it says, to 'wick moisture away from the skin keeping you cool and dry throughout your workout'. Your 'workout'. You're going to be 'working out'. Brilliant.

So you buy a Nike Sphere short-sleeve top (£25) and an Adidas Response zip fleece (£47) and Ronhill Advance Terraine long pants (£36) and Ronhill Advance shorts (£25).

That café in the park – is it open? It's almost exactly halfway round so would be the perfect place to stop and recharge. You'll need cash because it doesn't take cards. If you take coins they'll clank around in your pocket. (You've already got to take house keys and they're annoying enough.) But if you take a note, even a £5 note, you'll have the same problem because they'll give you change, probably quite a lot of change because you won't want much, only a coffee. Or a water. And maybe a pastry. Maybe.

*Just to illustrate the difficulty: 'Run To You' by Bryan Adams *isn't* a running song because if you tried to run to it, it would be with a curious galloping gait. Likewise 'Run To The Hills' by Iron Maiden. But 'Everybody Wants To Run The World' by Tears For Fears – they recorded it specially for Sport Aid in 1986 – is a running song. It just is.

'One of the many things nobody ever tells you about middle age is that it's such a nice change from being young'

Dorothy Canfield Fisher

Running: Pros and cons

Running suits the midlifer because:

• it provides an excuse to get out of the house, particularly at weekends, particularly if you've got kids;
• avoids the commitment issues and body consciousness that come with gym membership;
• requires very little imagination;
• it's sociable and therefore used by many women as a high impact alternative to coffee mornings and book groups;
• it's possible to be non-specific about the amount of effort required: 'going for a run' could mean a slow stumble round the park or a serious cross-country 5km-er;
• there are lots of cool accessories such as little sleeve pouches for your iPod, special water bottles with holes in the middle and nipple patches;
• it burns 100 calories per mile. Coincidentally, this is roughly the same amount of calories contained in a gin and tonic or a medium-sized glass of wine, effectively putting you in booze credit;
• it triggers the release of endorphins, chemicals released by the pituitary gland, which give a natural high, to which people sometimes become addicted. Endorphins are also released when having sex, eating sweets, taking drugs or eating spicy foods, listening to soothing music or when being tickled.

Bear in mind, however, that:

• you'll be seen in a public place wearing sports clothes (though at least you don't have to brave communal gym showers);
• it wrecks your knees (at least, that's our excuse);
• endorphins are also released at times of stress and pain.

MIDLIFE CLINIC: **SLEEP**

Yes, we know: you're just not sleeping as well as you used to. Mostly, this is because your partner gets up several times in the night to go to the toilet. When you confront him about it, which you do with a viciousness an onlooker might think disproportionate, he blames his prostate. And you know, he might be right, though it would help if he didn't insist on having a *fucking* coffee after dinner every *sodding* night.

In the paper the other day it said middle-aged men don't sleep as well as younger men because they don't have as much testosterone. Apparently, once men reach the age of 30, their testosterone levels start to drop at a rate of 1 to 2% each year. Perhaps this is worth mentioning? 'You're not sleeping because you're turning into a woman.' No – that wouldn't help.

Anyway, it's not just him. You're not sleeping either. Sometimes you wake up at 3am and can't get back to sleep because your brain is buzzing with thoughts such as:

- 'If I'm in the autumn of my years, who is going to rake up the leaves?'
- 'My father died four years before he reached my current age.'
- 'How come I can hear traffic? I never used to be able to hear traffic.'
- 'Maybe we should move somewhere where we can't hear traffic.'
- 'I'm sure my lymph nodes are bigger than normal.'
- 'What's that Philip Larkin poem about lying awake?'
- 'If I get cancer, I want to die at home.'
- 'If I get cancer, I need to convince myself and everyone around me that I'm not scared, I'm going to beat it, it's not going to kill me, etc. The problem is, *I can't do that.*'
- 'I wonder what the statistics are for breadmaker-related house fires? Memo to self: google tomorrow:

- 'I deserve to be loved more than I am.'
- 'I gave my children too much love.'
- 'You can never give your children too much love.'
- ' "Aubade"! That's it!'

If you are in a relationship and your partner is asleep next to you, you will also be thinking:

- 'Look at him, sleeping. Bastard. Why should he sleep? I'll wake him.'

MIDLIFE HERO:

Lee Child

In 1995, at the age of 40, Jim Grant was made redundant from his job as Presentation Director at Granada TV. He'd always had ambitions to write a novel – a commercial thriller, none of your literary nonsense. So he bought a pen and an A4 pad and set to work with 'a fury that was a perfect balance of creativity and financial necessity'. Killing Floor, his first book featuring the maverick ex-military policeman Jack Reacher, was published in 1997 under the pseudonym Lee Child. Within a year his immediate economic worries had receded. Within ten years he was a multimillionaire, with two Manhattan apartments and two houses in St Tropez, one each to live and write in.

Child attributes his success to his late-in-life career change: 'I was turning 40, and by that stage you are who you are. My tastes were developed. My needs were fixed. And you know, it wasn't a hobby. I was out of work. That made me a lot more realistic. I had no cherished preconceptions. The project was to write a book and make it sell or I would lose my house.'

9.
LAST ORDERS

While you've always known that the only certainty in life is death, midlife involves the shift from just knowing you are going to die sometime to becoming *truly aware of the inescapable fact of your own mortality;* the sort of infinite blackness that preoccupies you so entirely that it wakes you in the middle of the night in cold sweats, and has you counting the summers you've got left. Cheer up! At least you won't be around for the Band Aid centenary release.

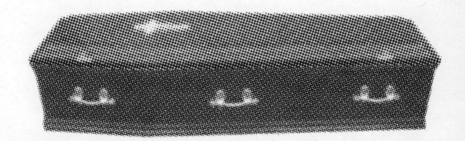

FUNERAL DOS AND DON'TS

Midlife means fewer weddings, more funerals. And not always for old people. Although we can't provide any deep and meaningful explanations for the howling injustice of it all, we can offer a few pointers on how to survive the actual event. (Well, not if you're the one in the coffin, obviously.)

Do:

- bring small children. Their presence is an affirmation of the circle of life, plus the sooner they are disabused of the notion that life is one long playdate and get to grips with their own mortality the better.
- pretend any hayfever symptoms from all the flowers are in fact an outpouring of grief (even though you never liked the bugger).
- use a venue's architectural merit for distraction and potential small talk at the wake (Edinburgh's Mortonhall Crematorium was designed by Sir Basil Spence, of Coventry Cathedral fame, and has 'Christine Keeler' chairs!)
- pre-read any chosen texts right to the end and between the lines for hidden meaning and potential misinterpretation that, if read at the service, could cause family rifts for generations.

Don't:

- wear black. It's terribly ageing.
- use the minute's silence to check your emails.
- cry too much. It causes puffiness and that undereye cream isn't cheap.
- drink more than everyone else at the wake. Alcohol will bring out the redness in your face, and it's unbecoming to be seen dancing on the table, especially if you're the widow.

After the event, **do** keep ashes well labelled and nowhere near the spice rack.

PARENTS, DEATH OF

Some believe we don't properly cross the Rubicon into middle age until our parents die. We may think we have mentally prepared for it (if we are lucky enough to have held onto our parents this far), yet beyond the straightforward business about just missing the person, it alters so much more.

It's different for us, different from how it was 30 or 40 years ago: we're the so-called 'sandwich generation', simultaneously raising children, working full-time and caring for ageing, dying parents. Nowadays, when a parent dies, it often marks the end of years and years of managed decline. For this reason it can be weirdly anti-climactic, a situation aggravated by grieving time being in short supply, especially if the other parent is still alive and your children are small.

Aside from the basic rawness and horror at the loss of the person who brought you into the world – a person you are statistically more likely to have had a brittle, compromised, awkward relationship with than loved uncomplicatedly – there's the terror of knowing that you have reached the top of the family tree. No longer is there the buffer of a generation between you and the end. YOU ARE NEXT.

- -

WILLS

So, yes. Making a will. Did you know the Law Society estimates that one in three people dies intestate? If this happens, you risk a big chunk of your estate going not to your spouse as you might have assumed but... Hey, look there, out of the window – can you see it? It's the most *extraordinary* chaffinch. I know! It's a breeding male with a little blue-grey cap and reddish... underparts. (Is that a word?) Anyway, sorry, where were we? Oh yes – wills.

Right. Remember the law doesn't recognise common-law spouses as equivalent to married couples or civil partners so…

Oh GOD it's so BORING make it STOP!! La la la la, Humpty Dumpty sat on the wall, ooh ooh fashion baby.

Look, all you need to know about wills is:

• You have to make one. You are going to die. And if you don't make one there'll be the mother of all unseemly squabbles after you're gone because the intestacy rules (google them) will kick in and your stepchildren will have to live on gruel and the decaffeinated Earl Grey you bought when you were pregnant ten years ago, which is still knocking around in your beverage cupboard. Yes, you have a 'beverage cupboard'. It was your idea, don't pretend it wasn't.
• You can make one yourself using a pre-printed form from a stationer, but don't because you'll probably screw it up – pets cannot be witnesses! – and your batty old aunt who lives in Australia and eats dingoes will inherit everything. Go to a solicitor.
• You need to think about giving stuff away as gifts to avoid inheritance tax (google it). Valuable stuff. And money. Horrible, isn't it?
• Once you've made it, store the will somewhere safe but accessible – not in a strongbox under the floorboards or behind a wall as in *The Borrowers*.
• You should include instructions for how you'd like your funeral. Remember, grief-stricken people need distractions. Don't be afraid to micro-manage. It's your funeral, no one else's funeral, etc, and your family will love spending hours going through iTunes on your laptop trying to find that Talking Heads song about heaven, or painting Celtic symbols onto the jute eco-coffin they had to drive up to Scotland to collect.

MIDLIFE QUIZ

Still ten minutes before *Midsomer Murders* starts? Here's something to do while you wait for the kettle to boil...

1 For your last birthday, your friends bought you:
a) a casserole dish
b) a whisky a third of your age
c) nothing: you've given up celebrating your birthday
d) a strippergram

alcohol

2 'My life so far has gone exactly according to plan, and I'm as successful as I always imagined I would be.' Do you:
a) disagree
b) strongly disagree
c) who are you kidding ✓
d) I'll get on with my life as soon as I've finished touring with my band/partying in Ibiza/backpacking across the Hindu Kush

3 Your friends are all:
a) getting divorced
b) secretly fantasising about getting divorced ✓
c) boasting about all the sex they've been having with athletic younger partners since they got divorced
d) Still optimistic about meeting Ms/Mr right

4 On a scale of 1–10, how tired are you right now?
a) 10
b) 9.5
c) 9
d) 5 or less ✓

5 How would you describe your current psychological state?
a) depressed
b) angry and resentful
c) uncontrollably reckless and impulsive
d) open-minded ✓

6 Teachers are:
a) stalwarts of the community
b) really young these days
c) paid more than you ✓
d) whingers who spend too much time in the pub: you know this because lots of them are your mates

7 What does dying mean to you? Is it:
a) something that happens to other people (albeit increasingly often) ✓
b) panic attacks, night sweats
c) that man in the cloak with the scythe
d) what you do to your hair

8 What keeps you awake all night?
a) the baby
b) money worries
c) all-night parties (the neighbours')
d) all-night parties (yours)
    sex ✓

9 Your ringtone is:
a) an old-fashioned telephone noise
b) Blondie's 'Call Me'/Lionel Richie's 'Hello'/Kraftwerk's 'The Telephone Call'
c) a voice recording of your children
d) in the charts ✓

10 A typical evening in is:
a) readymeal + glass of wine, DVD/current affairs programme + glass of wine, checking work emails + glass of wine ✓
b) dinner for eight, a really good wine you want to show off, the less-good wine your guests bring, digestifs, heated row about state v private education
c) feed kids, do kids' homework, bath kids, read to kids, feed partner, clear away supper, stay up past midnight writing business plan/novel/Open University essay dreaming that one day you'll be able to escape the lot of them
d) a Eurovision theme night

11 You think the type in this book is:
a) too small ✓
b) much too small
c) Futura, 11pt on 14pt – you can tell by the tails on the a's – though really you prefer Arial
d) cheaper to download and read electronically

12 While filling in this questionnaire you are:
a) listening to Radio 4 and waiting for the kettle to boil
b) simultaneously making the kids' packed lunch, ironing uniform and sending emails
c) commuting, because you had to live so far away from your workplace in order to afford a house
d) drinking tequila slammers, reading bits out loud and feeling smug about still being 'young'

At work skiing

- -

IF YOU ANSWERED:
Mostly **a**, **b** or **c** – Congratulations! Welcome to midlife!
Mostly **d** – It will get you in the end too, you know.

Jessica Cargill Thompson is a freelance writer and editor. In 2007, a mini midlife crisis prompted her to leave a great job as Deputy Editor of *Time Out London* in order to freelance, try new things, and be a better parent. Thanks to the recession, this proved to be a bad idea. In October 2009 she started the blog 'How to be Unemployed the White Collar Way'. She has edited several books for *Time Out*, and lives in south London with her husband and two children.

John O'Connell worked for years, far, far too long at the London listings magazine *Time Out*, where he was Books Editor. Since being made redundant on the grounds that 'no one really reads books any more', he has been writing, mostly about books, for *The Times*, the *Guardian*, *New Statesman* and the *National*. He is the author of *I Told You I Was Ill: Adventures in Hypochondria* (Short Books, 2005). He lives in south London with his wife and two children.